POST OFFICE DEPARTMENT
THIRD ASSISTANT POSTMASTER GENERAL
DIVISION OF STAMPS

✦

A Description of
United States Postage Stamps

Issued by the Post Office Department
from July 1, 1847, to December 31, 1936

WILDSIDE PRESS

Foreword

℀ Because of my belief in the values of philately, it is with the utmost pleasure that I dedicate to the stamp collectors of America this new booklet which contains for the first time reproductions of the postage stamps described therein.

℀ It is my sincere hope that the publication of these illustrations will contribute to a wider and more profound study of our postal issues, the designs of which portray the history and accomplishments of our great Nation.

James A. Farley

Postmaster General.

NOTICE

It is unlawful for any person to reproduce or photograph, or otherwise to copy, the illustrations of United States postage stamps contained in this booklet. It is also unlawful for any person to have in his possession plates for the making of such illustrations, or to make or have in his possession any plates from which reproductions, photographs, or copies of such illustrations can be made.

Section 150 of the Criminal Code (U. S. C., title 18, sec. 264) provides in part:

"* * * whoever by any way, art, or means shall make or execute, or cause or procure to be made or executed, or shall assist in making or executing any plate, stone, or other thing in the likeness of any plate designated for the printing of such obligation or other security [of the United States]; * * * or whoever shall have in his control, custody, or possession any plate, stone, or other thing in any manner made after or in the similitude of any plate, stone, or other thing, from which any such obligation or other security has been printed, with intent to use such plate, stone, or other thing, or to suffer the same to be used in forging or counterfeiting any such obligation or other security, or any part thereof; * * * or whoever shall print, photograph, or in any other manner make or execute, or cause to be printed, photographed, made, or executed, or shall aid in printing, photographing, making, or executing any engraving, photograph, print, or impression in the likeness of any such obligation or other security, or any part thereof, or shall sell any such engraving, photograph, print, or impression, except to the United States, or shall bring into the United States or any place subject to the jurisdiction thereof, from any foreign place, any such engraving, photograph, print, or impression, except by direction of some proper officer of the United States; * * * shall be fined not more than $5,000, or imprisoned not more than fifteen years, or both."

A DESCRIPTION OF UNITED STATES POSTAGE STAMPS ISSUED BY THE POST OFFICE DEPARTMENT FROM JULY 1, 1847, TO DECEMBER 31, 1936

INTRODUCTORY

The adoption of adhesive postage stamps in 1847, for use in the prepayment of postage on mail matter, represented one of the most important single improvements in the history of the Postal Service in America. As provided by law, these stamps were designed to be issued to postmasters on account, for sale to the public, thereby providing an accurate and automatic check on the postage revenues, in lieu of the less uniform and more uncertain methods that had prevailed in the past.

Prior to the issuance of the first stamps, letters accepted by postmasters for dispatch were marked "Paid" or "Due", by means of pen and ink or hand stamps of various designs. To facilitate the handling of mail matter, many postmasters provided special stamps or devices for use on letters as evidence of the prepayment of postage. These stamps of local origin were known as "Postmasters' stamps" or "Provisionals." After the introduction of postage stamps, these various methods of mailing without stamps affixed continued to be legal until the prepayment of postage by means of stamps of governmental issue was made obligatory by law, effective July 1, 1855.

As soon as possible after the enactment of the law on March 3, 1847, authorizing the issuance of adhesive postage stamps, contract was entered into with a private manufacturer for the printing of the quantities required for placing on sale July 1, following. Subsequent contracts for postage stamps continued to be awarded to private manufacturers until July 1, 1894, on which date the printing of stamps was transferred to the Bureau of Engraving and Printing, Treasury Department, where all postage stamps have since been produced.

SERIES OF 1847

Five-cent.—Portrait of Franklin after the painting by John B. Longacre, three-quarters face looking left, white neckerchief and fur collar to coat, the ground inclosure surrounded by a faintly engraved wreath of leaves, on which are the letters "U" and "S" placed in the left and right upper corners, respectively, and in each of the two lower corners a large figure "5." On a line curved with the upper portion of the medallion are the words "Post office", and following the lower line of the medallion outside the inclosure the words "Five cents." A border of fine straight lines surrounds the entire stamp. Color, light brown.

Ten-cent.—Portrait of Washington from Stuart's painting, three-quarters face, looking to the right, white neckerchief and black coat, faint wreath of artificial leaves surrounding the inclosing line of the medallion and extending to the border, on which are the letters "U" and "S" in the left and right upper corners, respectively, and in each of the lower corners a large Roman numeral "X". In a curved line around the upper and lower lines of the medallion are the words "Post office" at the top and "Ten cents" at the bottom, with a straight-line outer border, as shown on the 5-cent stamp. Color, black.

SERIES OF 1851

Denomination	Subject	Presentation	Color	Date of issue
1-cent	Franklin	Right	Blue	July 1, 1851
3-cent	Washington	Left	Red	July 1, 1851
5-cent	Jefferson	Right	Brown	Jan. 1, 1856
10-cent	Washington	Left	Green	May 10, 1855
12-cent	Washington	Left	Black	July 1, 1851
24-cent	Washington	Right	Lilac	June 14, 1860
30-cent	Franklin	Left	Orange	July 30, 1860
90-cent	Washington	Left	Blue	Sept. 5, 1860
1-cent carrier's stamp	Franklin	Left	Blue	Oct. 6, 1851
1-cent	Eagle	Left	Blue	Nov. 17, 1851

One-cent.—Profile bust of Franklin looking to the right, the words "U. S. postage" following an outside-border line in the medallion at the top, and "One cent" at the bottom in white capitals and on curved panels; on the corners and partly surrounding the two panels are convolute scroll-work ornaments, nearly meeting in points on the sides. Color, indigo blue. These were the first stamps in perforated sheets, and they were so issued as early as the 24th of February, 1857.

Three-cent.—Profile of Washington, after Houdon, facing left. Surrounding the ellipse is a tessellated frame, terminating in each of the four corners with a fine lathe-work rosette. At the top and bottom of the stamp are straight panels with a small part cut off at each end, the top bearing the words "U. S. postage" and the bottom "Three cents" in white capitals. In each of the four excised panel ends forming the extreme corners of the stamp is a small white diamond figure. A fine white line forms an outer rectangular border. Color, brick red.

Five-cent.—Portrait of Jefferson, after a painting by Stuart, three-quarters face, looking to the right and upon a ground slightly lighter than the general cast of the stamp. The lathe-work border nearly follows the rectangular outer lines of the stamp. It extends inward about ³⁄₁₆ of an inch wide, curving inward at the middle of the four sides, at the top and bottom touching the medallion and at the sides passing under it, thus leaving small spaces of a different figure at the four points outside the ellipse. This border follows the curved lines at the corners. It has slight projections on the outer side, equidistant from the corners. The words "U. S. postage" are in the middle of the border at the top, and "Five cents" at the bottom in white capitals follows the slightly curved line of the border. Color, brown.

Ten-cent.—Portrait of Washington, after the painting by Stuart, three-quarters face, looking to the left. Around the upper portion of the medallion, on a solid ground, are 13 five-pointed stars, above which, in a white panel following the general line of the medallion, are the words, in small stencil capitals, "U. S. postage", and at the bottom, in white capitals and following a double reverse curve, are the words "Ten cents." In each of the upper corners is the Roman number "X" in the nearly circular spaces left by the foliate and scroll ornamentations which appear there as well as, to a larger extent, in the trigonal spaces in the lower corners of the stamp. Color, dark green.

Twelve-cent.—Portrait of Washington, the same as on the 10-cent stamp. Above the medallion and conforming to its curve are the words "U. S. postage" in white shaded capitals, and below, similarly inscribed, are the words "Twelve cents." The medallion lies upon a rectangular, straight-line engraved background, whose corners which appear outside the ellipse are ornamented by scroll-work rosettes, and between this background and the outer border of the stamp there is a finely tessellated space. Color, black.

Twenty-four-cent.—Portrait of Washington after the same original as the 10- and 12-cent, but reduced to about two-thirds the size and facing three-quarters to the right. Double lines inclose the medallion, with a space sufficient between them to place at the top in white capitals the words "U. S. postage" and upon the lower half the words "Twenty four cents." These two inscriptions are separated on each side by rectangular ornaments with a white border and a white spot in the middle. Outside of this is intricate lathe work extending to the outer limit of the stamp, which has rounded corners and curved outer lines. Color, very dark lilac.

Thirty-cent.—Profile bust of Franklin looking to the left, slightly smaller, but evidently a reproduction, reversed, of that on the 1-cent stamp. At the top, following the elliptical lines of the medallion, is the word "Postage" in white capitals, and immediately above, reaching nearly to the border of the stamp, the letters "U. S.", and at the bottom "30" in Arabic numerals. On the left of the medallion is the word "Thirty" reading up, and on the right the word "Cents" reading down. In each corner is a shield with radiant lines extending from it into the corners, and bits of scroll work on each of the sides of the shield, the point of the shield being directed inward toward the center of the stamp. The irregular outer border terminates at each corner in two white spear points. Color, orange.

Ninety-cent.—Portrait of Washington in general's uniform, after the painting by Trumbull, three-quarters face. The tablet upon which this portrait appears is oblong, with an arched top, differing in this respect from any other stamp in the series. The ground is a deep, solid color and the picture occupies about one-half the opening. The words "U. S. postage", in white capitals, on a tablet following the arched line, appear at the top, and at the bottom, on a straight panel with rounded ends, are the words "Ninety cents." Outside the portrait inclosure, in the middle of each side, the frame appears to roll back, and there are some slight ornaments. Color, deep indigo blue.

One-cent carrier stamp.—Profile bust of Franklin, much like that on the 30-cent stamp, and looking to the left. At the top, on a straight line, in white capitals, is the word "Carriers", terminating at each end with a five-pointed star in heavy parentheses, and at the bottom in a straight line of white capitals, the word "Stamp", terminating also at each end with a white five-pointed star in heavy white parentheses. The corners of a straight rectangular figure, engraved in horizontal lines, appear from under the medallion and are marked by scroll-work rosettes. The remainder of the space inside the border lines of the stamp is in fine tessellated work. The value of the stamp is not stated, though it represented 1 cent. Color, indigo blue on rose-colored paper.

One-cent carrier stamp.—Picture of an eagle upon the branch of a tree, poised as for flight, looking to the left. The central portion of the ground is dark, shaded into white near the circumference. Within a dark border described by double lines there is a space left at the top for the words "U. S. P. O. despatch" in white capitals, and at the bottom "Pre-paid. One cent", the tablets on which these words appear not quite meeting on the left and right, leaving spaces of lighter color. Leaves of oak appear in the left-hand corners and of laurel in the right, clinging to the inscription surrounding the medallion, but leaving in the extreme corners a white ground. The longest diameter of the ellipse is horizontal. Color, light indigo blue.

STAMPS OF 1847 AND 1851 DEMONETIZED

These stamps are now obsolete and worthless for postage. A reasonable time after hostilities began in 1861 was given for the return to the department of all these stamps in the hands of postmasters, and as early as 1863 the Department issued an order declining to longer redeem them, the Confederate States having adopted their use, and so far as they could be reached in the hands of postmasters within the territory of those States, they were confiscated to the use of the Confederate postal authorities.

SERIES OF 1861—AUGUST 17, 1861, TO FEBRUARY 27, 1869

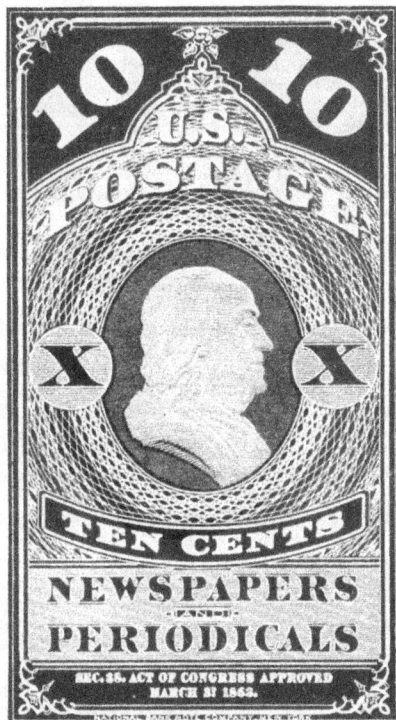

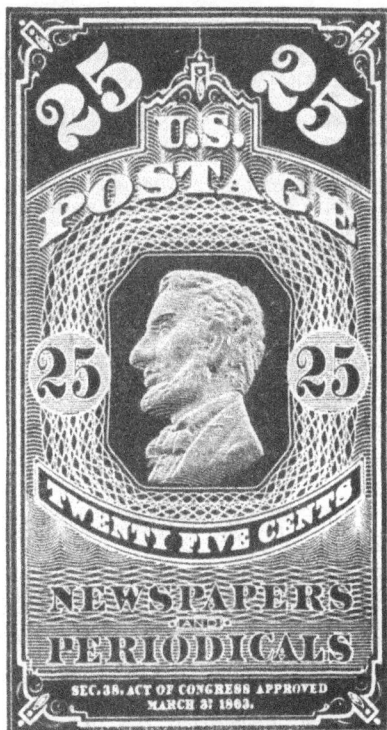

Denomination	Subject	Presentation	Color	Artist	Issued
1-cent	Franklin	Profile to right	Blue		Aug. 17, 1861
2-cent	Jackson	Full face	Black		July 6, 1863
3-cent	Washington	Profile to left	Rose	Houdon	Aug. 17, 1861
5-cent	Jefferson	¾ face to left	{Buff	Stuart	——— —, 1861
			{Brown	Stuart	——— —, 1862
10-cent	Washington	¾ face to left	Green	Stuart	Aug. 17, 1861
12-cent	Washington	¾ face to left	Black	Stuart	Aug. 17, 1861
15-cent	Lincoln	¾ face to right	Black	Photograph	June 17, 1866
24-cent	Washington	¾ face to right	Lilac	Stuart	Aug. 17, 1861
30-cent	Franklin	Profile to left	Orange		Aug. 17, 1861
90-cent	Washington	¾ face to left	Light blue	Trumbull	Aug. 17, 1861
5-cent (n. & p.)	Washington	Profile to right	Blue		
10-cent (n. & p.)	Franklin	Profile to right	Green		——— —, 1865
25-cent (n. & p.)	Lincoln	Profile to left	Red		

One-cent.—Profile head of Franklin, looking to the right, in an ellipse as large as could be placed upon the stamp, viz, 1 by ¾ inch. The entire ground within the inclosure is formed of lathe work. The outer ³⁄₁₆ of an inch of this space is more open. The upper corner spaces contain the Arabic figure "1", and the lower the white capital letters "U" and "S" in the left and right, respectively—all four corners having ornate surroundings. The words "U. S. postage" are placed above and "One cent" below the bust, following the curvature of the elliptic lathe work upon which they rest.

Two-cent.—A full face of Andrew Jackson fills the entire tablet, which is as wide as the stamp, three-fourths of an inch, and only ¹⁄₁₆ less in its long diameter than the stamp, ¹⁵⁄₁₆ of an inch, space being left at the top for the words "U. S. postage" above the elliptical ground, which is cross-hatched. The word "Two" and the distorted capital "U" in black fill the left lower corner, and the word "Cents" and a distorted "S" the right. An Arabic "2" in white is placed in each upper corner inclined outward to the left and right, respectively, and resting upon small black disks. Appropriate scroll decorations complete the upper part. The face of Jackson on this stamp is probably after the portrait by Dodge.

Three-cent.—A profile of Washington looking to the left rests upon an oblong tablet of lathe work, which is scarcely separated from the rest of the stamp by a border of lighter work of the same character. The entire ground of the stamp, except touches at and near the outer corners, is of this machine design. The large Arabic figure "3" appears in the upper corners, and between them in two lines are "U. S." and "Postage", the latter word taking the curve of the head close below. At the bottom, also in two lines of white capitals, are the words "Three" and "Cents", the ends of the lines tending upward. In the lower corners are the Gothic capitals "U" and "S", of the same size as the figures; all four are white, except slight tracery near the middle of each.

Five-cent.—A portrait of Jefferson rests upon a cross-hatched elliptical tablet ¹⁷⁄₃₂ by ⁴³⁄₆₄ of an inch. This is surrounded by a border of lathe work, principally in a triple-line design reaching the limits of the stamp and giving the general outline of a parallelogram, though the corners are rounded, and midway of each side it swells outward. A large white Arabic figure "5" is placed in each of the upper corners, and resting on each end of the line "U. S. postage", which rises in the middle to surmount the upper curve of the tablet. Similar white capitals form the words "Five cents" below the tablet, and the Gothic capitals "U" and "S", slightly distorted, are placed in the lower corners.

Ten-cent.—The head of Washington is upon a hatched ground whose cross lines are almost imperceptible, and is inclosed by four small white stars on each side, with the words "U. S. postage" above and "Ten cents" below. There are five more stars at the top of the stamp. The number "10", in Arabic figures, is placed in each upper corner, in an appropriate inclosure of ornamental design, and the white capitals "U" and "S" are seen in the left and right lower corners, respectively.

Twelve-cent.—The face of Washington is placed upon a cross-hatched elliptical ground ½ by ⅝ inch, which is surrounded to the edge of the stamp by a very fine geometrical design with a serrated outer white line, edged with a black hair line and the trace of an ornament in the middle of each side, with a larger one at each corner, outside the lines mentioned. The number "12", in Arabic figures, inclined as in the 2-cent stamp, is placed in each upper corner, with "U. S. postage" between, bordering the medallion line. Below, in the corners, are the white capitals "U" and "S", with the words "Twelve cents" just below the medallion line and rising at each end above the "U" and "S." The portrait is the same as that on the 10-cent stamp.

Fifteen-cent.—The portrait of Lincoln appears upon a cross-hatched elliptical ground ⁹⁄₁₆ by ¾ of an inch. On each side of this are fasces, and above are the words "U. S. postage" in white capitals upon a tablet curled at each end and encircling the number "15", in Arabic figures, in each upper corner; the figures lean outward to the right and left and backward. At the bottom are the words "Fifteen cents" in similar letters to those above and on a like ground, except that the latter terminates abruptly at the ends when reaching the fasces. The letters "U. S." in the lower corners are in bold-faced white capitals, the letters leaning to correspond with the numerals in the upper corners.

Twenty-four-cent.—The portrait is the smallest in the series and is inclosed by very fine lathe work ⅛ of an inch wide, the general outline of which is irregularly hexagonal. On each outer side, above the middle line, are four small five-pointed stars, enlarged in size from the lowest one up. At the top are three more stars, the smallest one in the middle. To the right and left of these, in the corners, and within an elliptical space, are the white-faced and shaded Arabic numerals "24", inclined slightly to the left and right. In each lower corner is a large five-pointed star, completing the 13; upon the left of these is the letter "U", and upon the right "S", tending inward at the top. Curled-leafed ornaments above and at the side of these stars complete the principal features of the stamp. The portrait ground is cross lined vertically and horizontally.

Thirty-cent.—The portrait is inclosed in a circle ²¹⁄₃₂ of an inch in diameter. The background of this space is obliquely cross lined at right angles. The inscriptions "U. S. postage" above and "Thirty cents" below the circle follow it closely; the number "30" leans outward in the upper corners, and the white capital letters "U" and "S" in the lower left and right hand corners, respectively, incline inward. Around the sides are scroll-work ornamentations.

Ninety-cent.—The portrait stands upon a background similar to that of the 5-, 12-, and 15-cent stamps. The border, about ³⁄₃₂ of an inch wide, is crossed with rays. The outer line of this border rises at the top to a Gothic apex. The denomination numerals "90" appear at each side of the tablet, on its border, one-fourth of an inch from its highest point. Across the top of the stamp, upon an independent pennant tablet, whose ends fall about the border, are the words "U. S. postage" in white, shaded capitals. The words "Ninety" and "Cents" are upon the left and right lower quarters of the border, which rests upon branches of oak and laurel tied with a small ribbon. The extreme lower corners are filled with the letters "U" and "S" in the left and right, respectively.

The 5-, 10-, and 25-cent newspaper and periodical stamps are alike in general style, 2 by 3¾ inches in dimension, the denominations being repeated in Arabic and Roman numerals, in the upper corners Arabic and midway of the sides Roman. The numbers "10" and "5", five-eighths of an inch high, are white-faced, while those at the side are the color of the stamp. On the 25-cent stamp the side figures are also Arabic. The numerals in the upper corners of the 10- and 25-cent stamps are inclined outward; those on the 5-cent are perpendicular.

The letters "U" and "S" appear near the top in horizontal line, and, immediately beneath, the word "Postage" in a line curved downward at each end. Next below this, in the middle of the stamp and surrounded by a border of lathe work, are the several profile medallion portraits in a misty style of engraving. The Washington medallion is circular, 1⅛ inches in diameter. The Franklin is an ellipse 1₁⁵₆ by 1₁⁵₆ inches, while the Lincoln is a parallelogram with clipped corners ⅞ by 1⅜ inches. Below the tablets are the words representing the denominations, and "Newspapers and Periodicals", in three lines. After this, reference is made as follows: "Sec. 38, act of Congress approved March 3, 1863." Below the border line proper—the heavy white line—at the bottom, in very small type, are the words "National Bank Note Company, New York."

The section (38) of the law referred to is found on page 707 of the Sixteenth Statutes: * * * "The Postmaster General may from time to time provide by order the rates and terms upon which route agents may receive and deliver at the mail car or steamer, packages of newspapers and periodicals delivered to them for that purpose by the publishers, or any news agents in charge thereof, and not received from nor designed for delivery at any post office."

The stamps were intended, therefore, to be purchased by publishers, that they might mail their publications where payment in money could not be made and the postage could not be collected at destination. The issue of these stamps began in the September quarter of 1865, and was terminated about February 1, 1869.

SERIES OF 1869—MARCH 1, 1869, TO APRIL 9, 1870

One-cent.—Head of Franklin, after bust by Houdon, looking to the left, surrounded by a circle of pearls; "U. S. postage" on a curved tablet at top, "One cent" on two similar tablets at bottom, with the numeral "1" in a small panel between the words. Color, Roman ocher.

Two-cent.—Post horse and rider, facing to left, surrounded by ornamental scroll work; "United States postage" on a fringed curtain at top, "Two cents" on a scroll at bottom, with large numeral "2" between the words. Color, light brown.

Three-cent.—Locomotive, heading to right, surrounded by ornamental scroll work; "United States postage" on a curved and a horizontal tablet at top; "Three cents" on wide curved tablets at bottom, with large numeral "3" between the words. Color, ultramarine blue.

Six-cent.—Head of Washington, after Stuart's painting, three-quarter face, looking to right; frame square, tessellated near the corners, with a circular opening, lined with pearls; "U. S." in upper left and right corners of frame, respectively; the word "Postage" in upper bar of frame; "Six cents" in lower, with the large numeral "6" between the words, and "United States" on each side. Color, ultramarine blue.

Ten-cent.—Shield, on which is resting an eagle with outspread wings, eagle looking to left; "United States postage" in upper section of shield with the number "10" below and the words "Ten cents" in a scroll at bottom; the whole design surmounted by 13 stars arranged in a semicircle. Color, orange.

Twelve-cent.—Ocean steamship, the S. S. *Adriatic*, surrounded by ornamental scroll work; "United States postage" at top; "Twelve cents" at bottom, with large numeral "12" between the words. Color, milori green.

Fifteen-cent.—Landing of Columbus, after the painting by Vanderlyn in the Capitol at Washington; ornamental scroll work at top and bottom; "U. S. postage" at top; "Fifteen cents" at bottom, with numeral "15" underneath. Colors: Picture, Prussian blue; scroll and ornamental work, light brown.

Twenty-four-cent.—Declaration of Independence, after the painting by Trumbull in the Capitol at Washington; ornamental and scroll work at top and bottom: "U" and "S" surrounded by circles at upper left and right corners, respectively; the word "Postage" between the two: "Twenty-four cents" in scroll at bottom, with numeral "24" underneath. Colors: The picture, purple lake; scroll and ornamental work, light milori green.

Thirty-cent.—Eagle, facing to left with outspread wings, resting on shield, with flags grouped on either side; the words "United States postage" in upper section of shield; the numeral "30" in lower; the words "Thirty cents" across the bottom; 13 stars arranged in semicircle at top of design. Colors: Eagle and shield, carmine; flags and other parts, blue.

Ninety-cent.—Head of Lincoln, from a photograph, in an ellipse, three-quarters face, looking to right, surrounded by ornamental and scroll work; numeral "90" at each of the upper corners; "U. S. postage" at top; "Ninety" and "Cents" in scroll at lower left and right corners of medallion, respectively; "U" and "S" in Old English text at lower left and right corners of stamp, respectively. Colors: Portrait in black; surrounding ornamental and scroll work, carmine.

The sizes of these stamps vary from the $13\frac{}{16}$ of an inch circle on the 1-cent to $13\frac{}{16}$ by $27\frac{}{32}$ of an inch in dimension.

The designs were furnished by the National Bank Note Co. of New York with their bid, upon which contract was entered into on the 12th of December, 1868.

ISSUE OF 1870—APRIL 9 TO 30

Denomination	Subject	Presentation	Original artist	Color
1-cent	Franklin	Left profile	Houdon	Blue.
2-cent	Jackson	Left profile	Powers	Brown.
3-cent	Washington	Left profile	Houdon	Green.
6-cent	Lincoln	Left profile	Volk	Red.
10-cent	Jefferson	Left profile	Powers	Chocolate.
12-cent	Clay	Left profile	Hart	Purple (neutral).
15-cent	Webster	Left profile	Clevenger	Orange.
24-cent	Scott	Left profile	Coffee	Purple (pure).
30-cent	Hamilton	Left profile	Ceracchi	Black.
90-cent	Perry	Left profile	Walcott	Carmine.

Additions and other changes

Date	Denomination	Subject	Presentation	Original artist	Color and note reference
Mar. 6, 1871	7-cent	Stanton	Left profile	Photograph	Vermilion, added. *a*
June 21, 1875	5-cent	Taylor	Full face	Daguerreotype.	Dark blue, added. *b*
June 21, 1875	7-cent	Stanton	Same added in 1870. Discontinued.		(*c*)
June 21, 1875	12-cent	Clay	Original issue of April, 1870. Discontinued.		(*c*)
June 21, 1875	24-cent	Scott	Original issue of April, 1870. Discontinued.		(*c*)
June 21, 1875	2-cent	Jackson	Original issue of April, 1870.		Changed to vermilion. *d*
Apr. 10, 1882	5-cent	Taylor	Original issue of June 21, 1875. Discontinued.		(*e*)
Apr. 10, 1882	5-cent	Garfield	Left, four-fifths face	Photograph	Chocolate brown. *e*
Oct. 1, 1883	2-cent	Washington	Left profile	Houdon	Metallic red. *f*
Oct. 1, 1883	4-cent	Jackson	Left profile	Powers	Green. *g*
Oct. 1, 1885	10-cent	Special delivery.	See note		Blue. *h*
June 11, 1887	1-cent	Franklin	Left profile		Light blue, new design.
Sept. 10, 1887	2-cent	Washington	Design of Oct. 1, 1883		Color changed to chrome green.
Sept. 23, 1887	3-cent	Washington	Design of April, 1870		Color changed to vermilion. *i*
Jan. 3, 1888	30-cent	Hamilton	Design of April, 1870		Color changed to brown.
Feb. 18, 1888	5-cent	Garfield	Design of April 10, 1882		Color changed to dark blue.
Feb. 28, 1888	90-cent	Perry	Design of April, 1870		Color changed to purple.
Sept. 6, 1888	10-cent	Special delivery.	Same as Oct. 1, 1885, except new wording.		(*h*)
Nov. 21, 1888	4-cent	Jackson	Design of Oct. 1, 1883		Color changed to carmine. *i*

For notes *a*, *b. c. d*, *e*, *f*, *g*, *h*, and *i*, see page 13.

One-cent.—A lined rectangular ground is left uncovered near the edges of the stamp on all sides. Inside this a more distinctly outlined border of scroll work and conventionally foliated ornaments fills the space to the medallion, which contains a profile bust of Franklin. The sides of this border are symmetrically curved inward, the corners being ornamentally rounded; on it, and resting upon and following the upper curve of the medallion, is a narrow panel bearing the words "U. S. postage." The words "One" and "Cent" in white capitals at the bottom appear in two curves, drooping at the ends and separated by an ornate heavy-faced white figure "1."

Two-cent.—An elliptical medallion, containing the profile bust of Jackson, after Powers's statue, rests upon a shield covering almost the entire stamp and placed upon a faint-lined rectangular ground. On this shield, above the medallion, is an ornamented tablet, curving with the ellipse except at the ends of the line, which tend outward, and bearing the words "U. S. postage." Faint trace of leafy branches curving upward fill the space at the bottom and sides of the shield not covered by the medallion. Across this, upon a ribbon-like double-curved tablet flowing at the ends, are the words, in white capitals, "Two" and "Cents", divided by the denomination figure "2."

Three-cent.—Nearly the whole face of the stamp is taken up by a shield resting upon a dimly lined ground, on which shield the bust of Washington, after Houdon's statue, in an elliptical opening, is placed, surmounted by a curved ornamented tablet bearing the words "U. S. postage." Under the portrait, on a flowing ribbon with forked ends, are the words "Three cents", separated by a large Arabic white-faced figure "3."

Six-cent.—On a delicately lined ground appears a dark rectangular mass of color, with heavy side projections nearly one-third of the length, on which is the bust of Lincoln in an elliptical medallion, surmounted by a panel bearing the words "U. S. postage." Below the medallion, on a waved ribbon with forked ends, are the words "Six cents", in white capitals, separated by a large white Arabic figure "6."

Seven-cent.—A large rectangular tablet, ornamented at the four corners with heavy balls, rests upon a background, the edges of which alone appear. On this tablet is an elliptical medallion containing the profile bust of Stanton, surmounted by a curved panel bearing the words "U. S. postage", while below the medallion is a similar panel bearing the words "Seven cents", in white capitals, separated by a white Arabic figure "7."

Ten-cent.—A large faint-lined shield rests upon a darker rectangular ground. On this shield is a profile bust of Jefferson, in an elliptical medallion, with words "U. S. postage" above and "Ten cents", separated by the number "10", below, displayed in the same way as the legends on the 6-cent stamp.

Twelve-cent.—On a lined rectangular frame is a raised panel of the same shape, with beveled edges. On this panel rests an elliptical medallion bearing the profile bust of Henry Clay. Above and below, in curved tablets, connected on the sides by triangular joints, are, respectively, the words in white capitals, "U. S. postage" and "Twelve cents", the two latter words being separated by the number "12" in Arabic figures. The words of denomination are of block letters.

Fifteen-cent.—On a lined rectangular frame, with triangular panels set in near each corner, is an elliptical medallion bearing the profile bust of Daniel Webster. Above, in a curved tablet, ending on either side in a circular knob, are the words, in shaded white letters, "U. S. postage." Below, in a similar tablet, but without knobs, in small white letters, are the words "Fifteen cents", separated by the number "15" in ornamented Arabic figures.

Twenty-four cent.—The denomination numerals, "24", in Gothic type, are in each of the upper corners, conforming in their position to the curve of an ornamental tablet, placed immediately above an elliptical medallion bearing a profile bust of Gen. Winfield Scott. Thirteen five-pointed stars are placed on this tablet; 2 at each end are blank white, while each of the 11 remaining bears a small Gothic capital letter, constituting the legend "U. S. postage" in the color of the stamp. The denomination is given at the bottom in small white Gothic capitals "Twenty-four" close up to and following the ellipse line, and "Cents" in a straight line, in the middle, below.

In the left lower corner appear a flag, loosely gathered around its staff, the muzzle end and part of the wheels of a piece of field artillery, and a pile of shells. In the right are three muskets stacked.

Thirty-cent.—On a rectangular-lined ground is placed a heavy beveled tablet, rounded in a half circle at the bottom, and with the upper corners described by bastion-like projections. From this point down to the half circle—a distance of half an inch—the tablet is straight lined on its sides and narrower than the stamp by about one-sixteenth of an inch. On the tablet is an elliptical medallion bearing the profile bust of Alexander Hamilton. The legend, "U. S. postage", above the medallion, is curved as on the 6-cent stamp, except that no panel incloses it, and the words "Thirty" and "Cents" appear in the black capitals at the bottom on a double-curved ribbon dropping inward with forked ends.

Ninety-cent.—The upper half of an elliptical medallion bearing the profile bust of Commodore Perry, is bounded by a rope attached at each end by eye-splices to a swinging panel describing the lower half of the ellipse, and bearing the words "Ninety" and "Cents" in block letters assigned to the left and right of the number "90." A plain tablet is the basis of the stamp, and is beveled except within $\frac{1}{8}$ of an inch of the corners, where it exhibits sharp edges. In each upper corner is a five-pointed star raised in the center, and in each lower corner the flukes of an anchor and part of the shank project from under the panel.

Five-cent (Taylor).—Tablet, legend, and denomination are of a style very similar to the 10-cent stamp. The portrait of Gen. Zachary Taylor is the only full face in the series. The dress is an open double-breasted military coat, within which appear the neck stock and high white collar.

Five-cent (Garfield).—On a rectangular-lined tablet, the greater portion of which is raised in the shape of a shield, is an elliptical medallion bearing the portrait of President Garfield. The medallion is bordered by a line of small white beads, the legend, "U. S. postage", being at the bottom of the stamp in small black block letters. The words "Five" and "Cents" are above the legend and partly on the lower edge of the tablet, divided by a large six-pointed star, upon which is the white-faced figure "5" upon a dark ground. The star is outlined with white, and the denomination words are each on lines curved downward at the ends.

Two-cent, 1883.—This is described in a circular of the Third Assistant Postmaster General, dated July 18, 1883: "* * * a plain tablet; above the oval, surrounding the head, are the words 'United States postage' and underneath the tablet are the words 'Two cents.'" It may be added that the tablet is shaped like the shield on the 3-cent stamp of this series and that the figure "2" separates the words "Two" and "Cents" which form a straight line resting partly on the point of the tablet and partly on the darkly shaded ground below. This is the first stamp of the series with the legend unabbreviated. The medallion is elliptical, and bears the profile bust of Washington.

Four-cent, 1883.—The tablet is rectangular and beveled, covering the entire stamp, the lower half in solid color. The legend, like that on the 2-cent stamp of even date, is in the unabbreviated form, "United States postage", following the upper line of an elliptical medallion bearing the profile bust of Andrew Jackson, and is in small white capitals. In each lower corner is a large white figure "4." Below these and in an unbroken straight line are the words "Four cents" in small white capitals with a very small star at the right and left and immediately under the figure "4."

One-cent, 1887.—A description by Postmaster General Vilas, given on the 23d of May, 1887, describes this stamp as "a profile bust of Benjamin Franklin upon a disk with shaded background, the lower portion of the oval disk being bordered with pearls, and the upper portion with a curved panel, containing, in small white letters, the words 'United States postage.' The whole is engraved in line upon a shield-shaped tablet with a truncated pyramidal base, bearing on it the words 'One cent' on either side of the figure 1." * * *

The changes of colors of other stamps of this series after June 11, 1887, were not accompanied by any change of design.

Ten-cent special-delivery, 1885 and 1888.—A line engraving on steel, oblong in form; dimensions, $\frac{13}{16}$ by $1\frac{1}{16}$ inches; color, dark blue. Design: On the left an arched panel bearing the figure of a mail-messenger boy on a run, and surmounted by the words "United States"; on the right an oblong tablet, ornamented with a wreath of oak and laurel surrounding the words "Secures immediate delivery at a special-delivery office." Across the top of the tablet is the legend "Special postal delivery", and at the bottom the words "Ten cents", separated by a small shield bearing the numeral "10."

The words "Secures immediate delivery at a special-delivery office" were changed, in 1888, to read "Secures immediate delivery at any post office." Both forms are valid.

NOTES

(a) The 7-cent Stanton was issued to meet the demand occasioned by a reduced rate of foreign postage under the postal treaty with the North German Confederation, effected in 1870.

(b) The 5-cent Taylor was issued for the new letter rate of postage under the convention of the General Postal Union adopted at Berne in 1874.

(c) The reduction of postage mentioned in note (b) requiring the 5-cent stamp, rendered the 7-, 12-, and 24-cent stamps unnecessary, and their issue was therefore discontinued.

(d) The vermilion of the discarded 7-cent Stanton stamp being now available, it supplanted the velvet-brown color on the 2-cent Jackson, which had given trouble from its similarity to that of the 10-cent Jefferson.

(e) Upon the death of President Garfield, a new design, quite exceptional, was made for the 5-cent stamp, and his portrait superseded that of Gen. Zachary Taylor, the blue color being displaced by a new one.

(f) This 2-cent Washington was adopted for use upon first-class matter, the rate upon which, under the act of March 3, 1883, was reduced from 3 to 2 cents a half ounce, and seemed to require a distinctive stamp. It superseded the Jackson vermilion 2-cent stamp.

(g) The Jackson profile, superseded, as stated, on the 2-cent stamp, was reengraved and given the green color and the 4-cent denomination, for use upon double-weight letters, under the act of March 3, 1883.

(h) This (special-delivery) stamp was an entirely new departure in style, as it was intended for use in executing a novel and, as it has proved, a successful experiment in postal delivery. In the act of Congress of March 3, 1885, page 387 of the Twenty-third Statutes, occur the following provisions:

"SEC. 3. That a special stamp of the face valuation of 10 cents may be provided and issued, whenever deemed advisable or expedient, in such form and bearing such device as may meet the approval of the Postmaster General, which when attached to a letter, in addition to the lawful postage thereon, the delivery of which is to be at a free-delivery office, or at any city, town, or village containing a population of 4,000 or over according to the Federal census, shall be regarded as entitling such letter to immediate delivery within the carrier limit of any free-delivery office which may be designated by the Postmaster General as a special-delivery office, or within 1 mile of the post office at any other office coming within the provisions of this section which may in like manner be designated as a special-delivery office.

"SEC. 4. That such specially stamped letters shall be delivered from 7 o'clock antemeridian up to 12 o'clock midnight at offices designated by the Postmaster General under section 3 of this act."

This delivery was extended by the act of August 4, 1886, to all post offices and to all mailable matter, thus giving rise to the change indicated by the Postmaster General on August 10, 1886: * * * "The words 'Secures immediate delivery at a special-delivery office' will, however, be changed to read 'Secures immediate delivery at any post office.' But as stamps with the former words are now in the hands of postmasters and the public, their use will continue until the present supply shall be exhausted."

Stamps of the first design lasted until September 6, 1888, when the stamp of that date was issued with the change, as directed, in the words on its face.

From January 24, 1893, to May 19, 1894, the special-delivery stamp was printed and issued in orange color, in connection with the Columbian stamps, and during that period no blue special-delivery stamps were issued.

(i) A change of color was rendered necessary in this case by the assignment of the green color to the 2-cent stamp, which had thus become the color of three stamps of the same series. More than a year later it was removed from the 4-cent stamp.

OFFICIAL POSTAGE STAMPS—1873–1884

The franking privilege having been abolished, to take effect on the 1st day of July, 1873, the Postmaster General, as required by law, provided a series of stamps of special design for each of the executive departments of the Government for the prepayment of postage on official matter. They are tabulated as follows:

Department, color, and denomination

Denomination	Subject	Executive (carmine)	State (green)	Treasury (velvet brown)	War (cochineal red)	Navy (blue)	Interior (vermilion)	Justice (purple)	Agriculture (orange)	Post Office (black); large Arabic numerals instead of faces
1	Franklin	$0.01	$0.01	$0.01	$0.01	$0.01	$0.01	$0.01	$0.01	$0.01
2	Jackson	.02	.02	.02	.02	.02	.02	.02	.02	.02
3	Washington	.03	.03	.03	.03	.03	.03	.03	.03	.03
6	Lincoln	.06	.06	.06	.06	.06	.06	.06	.06	.06
7	Stanton		.07	.07	.07	.07				
10	Jefferson	.10	.10	.10	.10	.10	.10	.10	.10	.10
12	Clay		.12	.12	.12	.12	.12	.12	.12	.12
15	Webster		.15	.15	.15	.15	.15	.15	.15	.15
24	Scott		.24	.24	.24	.24	.24	.24	.24	.24
30	Hamilton		.30	.30	.30	.30	.30	.30	.30	.30
90	Perry		.90	.90	.90	.90	.90	.90		.90
	Seward		2.00							
			5.00							
			10.00							
			20.00							
	Value of set	.22	39.00	2.00	2.00	2.00	.93	1.93	1.03	1.93

DESCRIPTION

The elliptical white ground filled by a face on the official stamps of the other departments is, on the stamps for the Post Office Department, made to represent the denominations by bold-face Arabic numerals $\frac{5}{16}$ of an inch high. The name of the department is printed across the top in lieu of the words "U. S. postage." There is also a slight difference in the ornamentation of the border.

In design, the official stamps for the other departments do not differ materially from those issued for sale to the public. The profile busts are retained; but each stamp has at the top the name of the particular department for which it was provided instead of the words "U. S. postage." Other changes, appearing in the border, need not be specified.

These stamps were supplanted on May 1, 1879, by the penalty envelope and on the 5th of July, 1884, were declared obsolete. (Sec. 3, p. 158, 23 Stat., amending sec. 3915 of the Revised Statutes.)

NEWSPAPER AND PERIODICAL STAMPS—JANUARY 1, 1875

1-, 2-, 3-, 4-, 6-, 8-, 9-, and 10-cent.—Allegorical figure of Freedom, looking to the right, and modeled after Crawford's statue upon the dome of the Capitol. The left hand rests on a shield and holds a wreath; the right grasps a sword. The head is adorned with a coronet of stars, surmounted by an eagle's head. The vignette stands in an arched frame, and at the top and sides are panels containing inscriptions: At the top, "U. S. postage"; at the bottom, words of denomination, also represented by Arabic figures in the upper corners; on the left side, reading upward, the word "Newspapers", and on the right, reading downward, the word "Periodicals." The lower corners are filled by shields. The color of these stamps is black.

12-, 24-, 36-, 48-, 60-, 72-, 84-, and 96-cent.—Vignette of Astræa, or Justice, in niche curved at the top, holding in her right hand the balance and resting with her left on a shield bearing the United States coat of arms. The figure is full robed, mailed, and girdled as to the upper part, and helmeted. Surmounting the helmet is an eagle with outstretched wings. Figures representing values on shields in upper corners; values also in sunken letters below, richly ornamented. Inscriptions on sides and at top in shaded capitals on lined ground. Color, pink.

One-dollar-and-ninety-two-cent.—Vignette of Ceres, Goddess of Agriculture, in curved niche. She holds in her left hand an ear of corn; her right, holding a wreath, rests against the hip. The figure faces to the front, and is clad in full, flowing robes. "U. S. postage" at the top; other inscriptions in italic letters on obelisks at either side, resting on lower slab containing value in white capitals. Value also in figures in upper corners. Color, deep brown.

Three-dollar.—Goddess of Victory, in curved niche, full-robed, girded, with sword to the left, and mantle thrown over shoulders. The right hand is stretched forward, holding a wreath; the left rests on a shield. Figures of value in upper corners; value below in letters on either side of a large figure "3." Inscriptions in solid labels on either side and on lined ground above. Color, vermilion.

Six-dollar.—Clio, the Muse of History, in curved niche, full robed, the toga thrown over the left shoulder. In her right hand she holds a stylus; in the left a tablet. Figures of value in upper corners, surrounded by curved ornaments. Inscriptions in white shaded letters on side, and above in dark letters on lined ground. Color, light blue.

Nine-dollar.—Minerva, the Goddess of Wisdom, full robed, in curved niche. The left hand is placed across her breast, holding a portion of her toga; the right is grasping a spear. Figures of value in upper corners. Inscriptions on sides in shaded italics, and above in small letters on lined ground. Value also in letters below on scroll. Beneath is a large "9" in curved ornaments. Color, orange.

Twelve-dollar.—Vesta, the Goddess of the Fireside, full robed, in curved niche. The left hand lifts her drapery; the right holds a burning lamp. Figures of value in upper corners on tablets; value also in letters on beaded frame beneath. Inscriptions in solid italic letters on sides and in small white letters above. Color, rich green.

Twenty-four-dollar.—Goddess of Peace, in curved niche—a partly robed figure, leaning against a broken column. She holds in her left hand an olive branch, while the right grasps three arrows. The value is in words beneath on a solid tablet; also in figures in ornamented curves in upper corners. Inscriptions in white shaded letters above and on sides, between which letters and each upper corner is a large six-pointed star. Color, purplish slate.

Thirty-six-dollar.—Figure representing Commerce, in full garments, in curved niche. She holds in her left hand the caduceus, the winged rod of Mercury; in her right, a miniature ship. Figures of value in upper corners and in ornamented capitals below. Inscriptions, also in ornamented capitals, on sides and above. Color, dull red.

Forty-eight-dollar.—Hebe, the Goddess of Youth, partly draped, in curved niche. The right hand holds a cup, which she is offering to the eagle, around whose neck is thrown her left arm. Figures of value on shields in upper corners, the word "Postage" between; value also in letters below in curved ornaments. The letters "U" and "S" in circles between lower corners and side inscriptions, the latter being in curved labels. Color, light brown.

Sixty-dollar.—Vignette of an Indian maiden standing in a rectangular frame. She is robed from her waist downward. Her right arm is extended, while her left hangs by her side. The background is a landscape, trees and vines to the left and wigwams to the right in the distance. Figures of value on shields in upper corners; value also in white letters on solid tablet below. Inscriptions in white on shaded labels on sides; at top, "U. S. postage" in white and purple. Color, rich purple.

The dimensions of all the above-described stamps are $\frac{18}{16}$ by 1⅜ inches.

These stamps were prepared by the Continental Bank Note Co. (then existing in New York, N. Y.) from designs selected in October, 1874. The act approved June 24, 1874 (sec. 6, p. 233, 18th Stats.), had prescribed the weighing in bulk of newspapers and periodicals presented by publishers and news agents for mailing and the payment of postage in advance by an "adhesive stamp" to be devised by the Postmaster General, the stamp to be affixed to the matter, "to the sack containing the same, or upon a memorandum of such mailing, or otherwise, as the Postmaster General may from time to time provide by regulation." He decided to attach the stamp to a memorandum. The law went into effect January 1, 1875.

Another section, 5, page 232 of the Eighteenth Statutes, fixed the rate of postage at 2 cents a pound upon weekly or more frequent publications and at 3 cents a pound for those issued less frequently. To meet the postage requirements stamps in the 2- and 3-cent denominations were provided. This was the advent of prepayment of postage upon printed matter in this manner. The stamps were sent to postmasters on the 11th of December, 1874, and at that time there were 35,000 post offices at which newspapers were received and 3,400 only at which they were mailed and prepaid under this law.

Under the law of March 3, 1879, page 359 of the Twentieth Statutes, the 3-cents-a-pound rate was repealed, and with it the 3- and 9-cent stamp issues were discontinued.

An act approved March 3, 1885 (p. 387 of the 23d Stats.), reduced the rate of postage on this second-class matter to 1 cent a pound when sent by publishers or news agents, and this gave rise to the 1-cent denomination of these stamps July 1, 1885, and the revival of the 3-cent denomination. The 9-cent was not, however, brought out again.

POSTAGE-DUE STAMPS—ISSUE OF 1879

[Act approved March 3 and made effective July 1, 1879]

Denomination	Color	First issued to postmasters—
1-cent	Light brown	May 9, 1879
2-cent	Light brown	May 9, 1879
3-cent	Light brown	May 9, 1879
5-cent	Light brown	May 9, 1879
10-cent	Light brown	Sept. 19, 1879
30-cent	Light brown	Sept. 19, 1879
50-cent	Light brown	Sept. 19, 1879

These stamps are alike except as to the denominations, which are expressed by Arabic numerals in the middle upon an elliptic ground of delicate lathe work. Upon the upper line of this ground are the words "Postage due" in white capitals; on the lower border is the denomination in letters of the same kind. On the left and right side, respectively, and separating these inscriptions, are the letters "U" and "S" upon white shields. There is a complex angular ornamentation of light line work surrounding this, and the whole rests upon a darker colored beveled tablet, of which but little can be seen, though it covers the entire stamp, which is an upright rectangle 1 by $\frac{22}{25}$ of an inch in dimensions. The color of all the stamps is light brown.

The color of these stamps was changed in 1889 to reddish brown and in 1891 the color was again changed to a bright claret. No change was made in the design.

ORDINARY POSTAGE STAMPS—ISSUE OF 1890

Denomination	Color	Subject	Placed on sale
1-cent	Blue	Franklin	Feb. 22, 1890
2-cent	Carmine	Washington	Feb. 22, 1890
3-cent	Purple	Jackson	Feb. 22, 1890
4-cent	Dark brown	Lincoln	June 2, 1890
5-cent	Light brown	Grant	June 2, 1890
6-cent	Light maroon	Garfield	Feb. 22, 1890
8-cent	Lilac	Sherman	Mar. 21, 1893
10-cent	Green	Webster	Feb. 22, 1890
15-cent	Dark blue	Clay	Feb. 22, 1890
30-cent	Black	Jefferson	Feb. 22, 1890
90-cent	Orange	Perry	Feb. 22, 1890

NOTE.—The 8-cent stamp was not issued until Mar. 21, 1893, in connection with the reduction of the registry fee from 10 to 8 cents.

One-cent.—Profile bust, after Ceracchi, of Benjamin Franklin, looking to the left, on an ellipse, with dark background and narrow white border, immediately above which, set in a panel conforming to the elliptical curve, are the words "United States postage" in white capitals, and below which, in slightly larger and shaded letters, arranged in a waved line running nearly the whole width of the stamp, are the words "One cent." Just above these latter words, on either side, is a white numeral of denomination—the Arabic figure "1"—in a small oval space, surrounded by an ornate scroll, the upper portion of which is connected with and serves as a support to the panel around the medallion. The whole is placed upon a distinctly lined oblong tablet, seven-eighths of an inch high by three-fourths of an inch wide, with beveled sides and bottom. The color is blue. The medallions on all this series are elliptical.

Two-cent.—Profile bust, after Houdon, of George Washington, looking to the left. The surroundings of the medallion are the same as in the 1-cent stamp, with the necessary change of figures and letters representing the denomination. Color, carmine. An improved quality of color for the 2-cent stamp was adopted May 12, 1890.

Three-cent.—Profile bust, after Powers, of Andrew Jackson, looking to the left. The surroundings of the medallion are the same as in the 1-cent stamp, with the necessary change of figures and letters representing the denomination. Color, purple.

Four-cent.—Portrait of Abraham Lincoln, after a photograph from life, three-quarters face, looking to the right. The surroundings of the medallion are the same as in the 1-cent stamp, with the necessary change of figures and letters representing the denomination. Color, dark brown. Issued June 2, 1890.

Five-cent.—Portrait of U. S. Grant, after a photograph from life, three-quarters face, looking to the right. The surroundings of the medallion are the same as in the 1-cent stamp, with the necessary change of figures and letters representing the denomination. Color, light brown. Issued June 2, 1890.

Six-cent.—Portrait of James A. Garfield, after a photograph from life, three-quarters face, looking to the left. The surroundings of the medallion are the same as on the 1-cent stamp, with the necessary change of figures and letters representing the denomination. Color, light maroon.

Eight-cent.—Portrait of Gen. William T. Sherman, after a photograph from life, full face. The surroundings of the picture are the same as those on the stamps below the 10-cent denomination, with the necessary change of figures and letters representing the value. Color, lilac. It was issued March 21, 1893, in connection with the reduction of the registry fee from 10 to 8 cents.

Ten-cent.—Portrait of Daniel Webster, after a daguerreotype from life, three-quarters face, looking to the left, with dark background and narrow white border, around the upper half of which, set in a panel conforming to the medallion curve, are the words "United States postage" in small white capitals, the words "Ten cents" in somewhat similar letters being placed in a like panel below the medallion. Below this again, in the two lower corners of the stamp, are plain Arabic numerals of denomination, "10", set in circular spaces surrounded with ornate scrolls not unlike those in the 1-cent stamp. The whole is placed upon an oblong tablet, ⅞ of an inch high by ¾ of an inch wide, with beveled sides and bottom. The color is green.

Fifteen-cent.—Portrait of Henry Clay, after a daguerreotype from life, three-quarters face, looking to the left. The surroundings of the medallion are substantially the same as in the 10-cent stamp, with appropriate changes of figures and letters representing the denomination. Color, deep blue.

Thirty-cent.—Profile bust of Thomas Jefferson, after Ceracchi, looking to the left. The surroundings of the medallion are the same as in the 10-cent stamp, with the necessary change of the letters and figures of denomination, the latter, however, being of block form. Color, black.

Ninety-cent.—Profile bust of Commodore O. H. Perry, after Wolcott's statue, looking to the left. The surroundings of the medallion are substantially the same as in the 30-cent stamp, with the necessary change of the letters and figures of denomination. Color, orange.

The dimensions of all the above stamps are three-fourths by seven-eighths of an inch.

SPECIAL DELIVERY STAMP (10-CENT)—ISSUE OF 1893

As the special-delivery stamp closely resembled the 1-cent and 4-cent Columbian stamps, giving rise to mistakes in the payment of postage and the treatment of mail matter, its color was changed from blue to orange January 24, 1893, and so continued to January 5, 1894, when the printing in blue was resumed. The issue of the orange-colored special-delivery stamp was not discontinued until May 19, 1894, when the stock on hand at the manufactory was exhausted.

There were 5,099,500 special-delivery stamps of the orange color issued to postmasters.

COLUMBIAN SERIES OF POSTAGE STAMPS—ISSUE OF 1893

The department placed upon sale on Monday, January 2, 1893, at post offices throughout the country, a new series of postage stamps (not including the 8-cent denomination, issued later) and stamped envelopes, known as the Columbian series. The issue of these stamps ceased April 12, 1894.

Denomination	Color	Subject	Placed on sale
1-cent	Blue	Columbus in sight of land	Jan. 2, 1893
2-cent	Purple maroon	Landing of Columbus	Jan. 2, 1893
3-cent	Green	Flag ship of Columbus	Jan. 2, 1893
4-cent	Blue	Fleet of Columbus	Jan. 2, 1893
5-cent	Chocolate brown	Columbus soliciting aid of Isabella	Jan. 2, 1893
6-cent	Purple	Columbus welcomed at Barcelona	Jan. 2, 1893
8-cent	Magenta	Columbus restored to favor	Mar. 3, 1893
10-cent	Dark brown	Columbus presenting natives	Jan. 2, 1893
15-cent	Dark green	Columbus announcing his discovery	Jan. 2, 1893
30-cent	Sienna brown	Columbus at La Rabida	Jan. 2, 1893
50-cent	Slate blue	Recall of Columbus	Jan. 2, 1893
$1	Salmon	Isabella pledging her jewels	Jan. 2, 1893
$2	Mineral red	Columbus in chains	Jan. 2, 1893
$3	Yellow green	Columbus describing third voyage	Jan. 2, 1893
$4	Carmine	Isabella-Columbus	Jan. 2, 1893
$5	Black	Columbus	Jan. 2, 1893

The Columbian stamps were issued in the denominations of 1, 2, 3, 4, 5, 6, 8, 10, 15, 30, and 50 cents, and of $1, $2, $3, $4, and $5. These stamps differ in size and form from those of the 1890 series, the engraved space being $7/8$ by $1^{11}/_{32}$ inches, each stamp bearing a design commemorative of the discovery of America by Columbus.

The stamps are executed from line engravings on steel, the general design of the upper portion of all of them being substantially the same. The details of this design are, first, a white-faced imprint of the years "1492" and "1892", in the upper left- and right-hand corners, respectively; then in white-shaded capitals beneath, in a waved line, the words "United States of America", below which, in a narrow tablet conforming to the curved frame of the picture under it, are the words of denomination; for example, "Postage, two cents", "Postage, two dollars", etc. These words end on either side of the stamp in a space of circular form with ornamental surroundings, within which are Arabic numerals of value—standing alone in the case of denominations under $1, but accompanied by the dollar mark in denominations of $1 and upward, as "2" (meaning cents), $2, etc. Underneath all this is the scene represented, inclosed in a plain white frame with arched top, extending nearly the entire length of the stamp, and taking up in every case probably three-fourths of its whole face, the appropriate designation of the picture being given in small white capitals at the bottom. The scenes represented are these:

One-cent.—Columbus in Sight of Land, after the painting by William H. Powell. This reproduction is inclosed in a circle. On the left of it is represented an Indian woman with her child, and on the right an Indian chief with headdress of feathers—each figure in a sitting posture. Color, Antwerp blue.

Two-cent.—Landing of Columbus, after the painting by Vanderlyn, in the Rotunda of the Capitol at Washington. Color, purple maroon.

Three-cent.—Flagship of Columbus, the *Santa Maria*, in mid-ocean, from a Spanish engraving. Color, medium shade of green.

Four-cent.—Fleet of Columbus, the three caravels, *Santa Maria*, *Nina*, and *Pinta*, from a Spanish engraving. Color, ultramarine blue.

Five-cent.—Columbus Soliciting Aid of Isabella, after the painting by Brozik, in the Metropolitan Museum of Art in New York City. Color, chocolate brown.

Six-cent.—Columbus Welcomed at Barcelona, scene from one of the panels of the bronze doors by Randolph Rogers in the Capitol at Washington. On each side of the scene represented is a niche, in one of which is a statue of Ferdinand and in the other a statue of Balboa. Color, royal purple.

Eight-cent.—Columbus Restored to Favor, after a painting by Jover. Color, magenta red. Issued March 1, 1893.

Ten-cent.—Columbus Presenting Natives, after the painting by Luigi Gregori, at the University of Notre Dame, South Bend, Ind. Color, Vandyke brown.

Fifteen-cent.—Columbus Announcing His Discovery, after the painting by R. Baloca, now in Madrid. Color, dark green.

Thirty-cent.—Columbus at La Rabida, after the painting by R. Maso. Color, sienna brown.

Fifty-cent.—Recall of Columbus, after the painting by A. G. Heaton, now in the Capitol at Washington. Color, slate blue.

One-dollar.—Isabella Pledging Her Jewels, after the painting by Munoz Degrain, now in Madrid. Color, rose salmon.

Two-dollar.—Columbus in Chains, after the painting by Luetze, now in Providence, R. I. Color, toned mineral red.

Three-dollar.—Columbus Describing Third Voyage, after the painting by Francisco Jover. Color, light yellow green.

Four-dollar.—Portraits in circles, separated by an ornate device, of Isabella and Columbus, the portrait of Isabella after the well-known painting in Madrid, and that of Columbus after the Lotto painting. Color, carmine.

Five-dollar.—Profile of head of Columbus, after a cast provided by the Treasury Department for the souvenir 50-cent silver piece authorized by act of Congress. The profile is in a circle, on the right of which is the figure of America, represented by an Indian woman with a crown of feathers, and on the left a figure of Liberty, both figures being in a sitting posture. Color, black.

ORDINARY POSTAGE STAMPS—1894

Denomination	Face	Color	Date of issue	On water-marked paper after—
1-cent	*Franklin*	*Blue*	*Oct. 10, 1894*	*Apr. 29, 1895*
1-cent	Franklin	Green	Jan. 17, 1808	Jan. 17, 1898
2-cent	Washington	Carmine	Oct. 5, 1894	May 2, 1895
3-cent	Jackson	Purple	Sept. 24, 1894	Oct. 31, 1895
4-cent	*Lincoln*	*Velvet brown*	*Sept. 11, 1894*	*June 5, 1895*
4-cent	Lincoln	Red brown	Oct. 7, 1898	Oct. 7, 1898
5-cent	*Grant*	*Light brown*	*Sept. 28, 1894*	*June 11, 1895*
5-cent	Grant	Blue	Mar. 8, 1898	Mar. 8, 1898
6-cent	*Garfield*	*Light maroon*	*July 18, 1894*	*Aug. 31, 1895*
6-cent	Garfield	Magenta	Dec. 31, 1898	Dec. 31, 1898
8-cent	Sherman	Lilac	Mar. 25, 1895	July 22, 1895
10-cent	*Webster*	*Milori green*	*Sept. 17, 1894*	*June 7, 1895*
10-cent	Webster	Light brown	Nov. 11, 1898	Nov. 11, 1898
10-cent	Special-delivery messenger boy	Blue	Oct. 10, 1894	Aug. 16, 1895
15-cent	*Clay*	*Deep blue*	*Oct. 15, 1894*	*Sept. 10, 1895*
15-cent	Clay	Olive green	Nov. 30, 1898	Nov. 30, 1898
50-cent	Jefferson	Orange	Nov. 1, 1894	Nov. 9, 1895
$1	Perry	Black	Nov. 15, 1894	Aug. 12, 1895
$2	Madison	Sapphire blue	Dec. 10, 1894	Aug. 13, 1895
$5	Marshall	Gray green	Dec. 10, 1894	Aug. 16, 1895

Those stamps given in *italics* were changed in color only, as shown in the next line below that italicized.

Prior to July 18, 1894, there were no ornaments in the upper corners of the stamps. In this series the 30-cent and 90-cent stamps heretofore available have been superseded by stamps in the 50-cent and $1 denominations.

The introduction of these stamps followed the transfer of the manufacture of stamps from private contractors (the American Bank Note Co.) to the Treasury Department in July, 1894. The changes are so slight that no notice beyond that given above is necessary, except, perhaps, as to the special-delivery stamp, which, to distinguish it from that made by private contractors, has a small line under the words "Ten cents".

POSTAGE-DUE SERIES OF 1894

The dimensions of the postage-due stamps were lessened when the Treasury Department assumed the manufacture of stamps in 1894, and the color was deepened to a deep claret, with smaller white numerals than had been used up to that time. The two elliptical lines inclosing the numerals, and between which the words "Postage due", the letters "U. S.", and the denomination were written in words, entirely disappeared on the lower half of the new stamp. The words "Postage due" remained in a similar position as on the original stamp, but the words of denomination described a double curved line at the bottom (as in the current regular issue below the 10-cent denomination). The initials "U" and

"S" were moved to the left and right upper corners, respectively, and the tablet bearing the white figure of denomination is a four equi-sided scalloped figure of lathe work, with the greatest diameters vertical and horizontal. The exact dates of introduction and first use of watermarked paper in their manufacture are as follows:

Denomination	Color	Date of issue	On water-marked paper after—
1-cent	Deep claret	Aug. 14, 1894	Aug. 29, 1895
2-cent	Deep claret	July 20, 1894	Sept. 14, 1895
3-cent	Deep claret	Apr. 27, 1895	Oct. 30, 1895
5-cent	Deep claret	Apr. 27, 1895	Oct. 15, 1895
10-cent	Deep claret	Sept. 24, 1894	Sept. 14, 1895
30-cent	Deep claret	Apr. 27, 1895	Aug. 21, 1897
50-cent	Deep claret	Apr. 27, 1895	Mar. 17, 1896

The old stamps were 1 by $25/32$ of an inch in size. Their successors, mentioned above, are $7/8$ by $23/32$ of an inch.

NEWSPAPER AND PERIODICAL STAMPS OF 1895

On February 1, 1895, a new series of these stamps was introduced, retaining the central allegorical illustrations, reduced and surrounded by new designs by the Bureau of Engraving and Printing, by which they were engraved and printed. The denominations of these stamps, from 1 to 10 cents, inclusive, are of the same design. The numerals in the upper corners are of equal size in the 1-, 2-, and 5-cent stamps, while those in the 10-cent stamp are condensed so as to fill the same space that is given to the others, besides being slightly different in style. Those in the 1- and 5-cent denominations are shaded dark on the lower half; those of the 2- and 10-cent stamps are white faced. The statue of Freedom, by Crawford, is that which surmounts the Dome of the Capitol at Washington, and is the same on the 1-, 2-, 5-, and 10-cent stamps. The same subject was used on the lower denominations of the old series, but the representation on the new stamps is full face.

The inscription "U. S. postage" at the top of the stamps is in white block letters upon an arched line, and the words "Newspapers" on the left and "Periodicals" on the right are in vertical lines. The denominations at the bottom are in white Roman letters, and there is foliate ornamentation in the lower corners. The upper border line of the 25- and 50-cent stamps is broken by two indentations, separating that border into three equal parts, and the side inscriptions follow a curved line upon a scroll. The dimensions of the stamps below the $2 denomination are $\frac{3}{4}$ by 1$\frac{3}{8}$ inches. The remaining denominations from $2 to $100 are of the same size as the stamps of the retired series—that is to say, $\frac{15}{16}$ by 1$\frac{3}{8}$ inches. Other facts as to this series are shown in this table:

Denomination	Color	Figure	On water-marked paper after—
1-cent	Black	Freedom	Jan. 11, 1896
2-cent	Black	Freedom	Nov. 21, 1895
5-cent	Black	Freedom	Feb. 12, 1896
10-cent	Black	Freedom	Sept. 13, 1895
25-cent	Pink	Astræa	Oct. 11, 1895
50-cent	Pink	Astræa	Sept. 19, 1895
$2	Orange	Victory	Jan. 23, 1897
$5	Blue	Clio	Jan. 16, 1896
$10	Green	Vesta	Mar. 5, 1896
$20	Slate	Peace	Jan. 27, 1896
$50	Carmine	Commerce	July 31, 1897
$100	Purple	Indian	Jan. 23, 1896

The use of newspaper and periodical stamps was discontinued on July 1, 1898. They no longer have any postage value, and those in the hands of postmasters at that time were ordered to be returned for credit.

For the benefit of collectors 50,000 sets of these 1895 stamps were placed on sale at the first-class post offices at $5 a set, and at that rate there were about $110,000 worth disposed of up to the date of their withdrawal, in January, 1899.

TRANS-MISSISSIPPI-"OMAHA" EXPOSITION STAMPS OF 1898

Denomination	Subject of illustration	Color
1-cent	Marquette on the Mississippi	Dark green.
2-cent	Farming in the West	Copper red.
4-cent	Indian hunting buffalo	Orange.
5-cent	Fremont on Rocky Mountains	Dark blue.
8-cent	Troops guarding train	Dark lilac.
10-cent	Hardships of emigration	Slate.
50-cent	Western mining prospector	Olive.
$1	Western cattle in storm	Black.
$2	Mississippi River bridge	Light brown.

The issue of these stamps began June 10 and ceased December 31, 1898.

The engraved surface of these stamps is ⅞ by 1¹¹⁄₃₂ inches, with the longest side horizontal. The denominations are in Arabic numerals, repeated upon shields in the upper corners. The 1-cent figure is exceptional in having a double border line, and the 10- and 50-cent are shown in more condensed numerals than those on the other stamps, and are of the Gothic type. Both numerals and letters are in white, and the dollar mark is included on these stamps with the numerals upon the elliptical tablet of the shield. The illustrations are within an inclosure resembling that of the letter "C" slightly condensed and recumbent, with the open side up and the opening filled by a curved panel upon which are the words "United States of America." On the lower border of this inclosure are the words, in very small letters, describing the picture above, and at the bottom of the stamp, in a straight line, are the words of denomination. All but the descriptions of the illustrations, which are in Gothic, are in Roman letters. Maize and wheat designs fill the lower corners and upper interstices. All the lettering is in capitals.

The designs for these stamps, which were executed by the Bureau of Engraving and Printing, were as follows:

One-cent.—"Marquette", a painting, by Lamprecht.

Two-cent.—"Farming in the West", a photograph.

Four-cent.—"Indian hunting buffalo", an engraving in Schoolcraft's history of the Indian tribes.

Five-cent.—"Fremont on the Rocky Mountains", an old engraving.
Eight-cent.—"Troops guarding train", a drawing, by Frederic Remington.
Ten-cent.—"Hardships of emigration", painting, by A. G. Heaton.
Fifty-cent.—"Mining prospector", a drawing, by Frederic Remington.
One-dollar.—"Cattle in a storm", J. MacWhirter.
Two-dollar.—"Mississippi River Bridge at St. Louis", photograph.
These stamps were first placed on sale June 10, 1898, at Omaha, Nebr.

PAN-AMERICAN STAMPS OF 1901

The stamps of this series were placed on sale at post offices May 1, 1901, and were withdrawn from sale October 31, 1901, the dates fixed for the opening and closing of the Pan-American Exposition at Buffalo, which they were issued to commemorate.

The stamps are described as follows:

Denomination	Subject	Color	Legend
1-cent	Lake steamer	Green and black	Fast lake navigation.
2-cent	Railway train	Red and black	Fast express.
4-cent	Automobile	Brown and black	Automobile.
5-cent	Steel-arch bridge	Blue and black	Bridge at Niagara Falls.
8-cent	Ship-canal locks	Lilac and black	Canal locks at Sault Ste. Marie.
10-cent	Ocean steamship	Light brown and black	Fast ocean navigation.

These stamps are of uniform dimensions, $\frac{76}{100}$ by $\frac{19}{100}$ of an inch, the longer side being horizontal. The borders take the colors of the regular series on the same denominations at this date. The words "Commemorative series, 1901", and "United States of America" next below appear above the vignette; the legend in a line next below the central opening, with the denomination in a line at the bottom, appears in the same order on all stamps of the series. All the lettering is in white Roman capitals. The numerals are all white-faced Arabic in the Roman type except the 10-cent, which is the block-letter type of figure condensed to secure space for the two figures. The borders are well separated from the central pictures, and the words of denomination at the bottom are preceded on the same line by the word "Postage." All the central illustrations are from photographs and are printed in black.

One-cent.—The lake steamer presents the port bow. It has but one funnel. The pilot house is well forward. The vessel is propelled by side wheels. The vignette is within an elliptical opening whose greatest diameter is horizontal. On either side are fluted columns whose bases are draped in form of shields, upon which, in pear-shaped inclosures, appears the figure of denomination, "1." On an entablature, which rests upon the columns and extends across the top of the stamp, is the general device "Commemorative series, 1901", and beneath it "United States of America." A trigonal panel fills the upper corners between the opening and the capitals of the columns. The legend follows the lower line of the ellipse and the words of denomination follow in a line below. The spaces on either side below the opening and above the words of denomination are filled with foliate scroll work.

Two-cent.—The train of four cars is drawn by a four-driver locomotive. Four parallel tracks are shown. The vignette ground is oblong, the ends being rounded and the upper and lower sides projecting at the point of greatest diameter of the end curves and where the two meet in a corner. This upper line is slightly arched, while the lower line is straight and horizontal. The upper line of the border rises in the middle to conform to the opening below, and the device appears following this border line, outside of it. The words "United States of America" appear in two lines of two words each in the space between the border line and the opening, or ground for the vignette. Leaning on the curved lines at each end of the opening is a winged female figure bearing a torch, and beneath this figure in each lower corner is the denominational numeral. The legend "Fast express" and the words of denomination are located as in the 1-cent stamp. This may be said of the rest of the series.

Four-cent.—The automobile is of the closed-coach order, with two men on the box and a part of the United States Capitol at Washington as a background. An oblong opening is provided for the vignette. The corners of this space are broken, with an entering curve on the lower angles and clipped with re-entrant angles at the top; the upper line is also slightly arched. Immediately above this, on a panel, following the curvature of the opening, rounded at the right-hand end and scrolled at the other, appear the words "Of America", while immediately above this, with an opposite curvature, are the words "United States." The device is given on the cornice ornament, the upper part of the border being an architectural cornice design. The numeral "4" is just outside the lower corners of the vignette opening, and room is made for them by the entering curves which clip its lower corners. The legend "Automobile" appears on a panel, but the words of denomination are on the open ground of the border.

Five-cent.—This depicts the large single-span steel bridge below Niagara Falls. Two trolley cars are seen upon it, and a view of the Falls is shown under, beyond, and up the river, with the graceful springing arch as a frame. The opening for the illustration is much like that of the 4-cent stamp, except that the upper corners are notched in at right angles, and the lower corners have two such entering angles, which connect with the lower straight horizontal line of the opening by a curve. The upper line of the opening describes a higher curve than that of the 4-cent stamp, and the words "United States of America", in one line, follow this curve and are immediately above it. Above these words, in a straight line, is the device, thus leaving a space in the upper corners, which is filled with a trigonal panel. The sharp angular shields bearing the figure of denomination are placed just outside the opening, midway of the ends, and upon fasces with battle-axes cutting outward. The legend is on a panel, while the words of denomination are on the general ground.

Eight-cent.—The great ship-canal locks at Sault Ste. Marie, Mich., including the immediate surroundings, are given in a view from a higher point. The opening is an arch, cut at bottom just below the greatest horizontal diameter, while, though the ornamentation dims a part of the figure, the entire border is of a shieldlike design, its superior members being quite distinct. Small shields pendent by a cord from the upper corners bear the numeral "8" on each side. Delicate crinkled ribbon ornaments are seen at the top of the border to fill out the inward curve spaces of the shield. The legend at the bottom and words of denomination are each upon separate panels.

Ten-cent.—An American Line steamship with two smokestacks and masts presents its starboard bow lapped by a rising wave. The general outline of the opening is that of an arch, connected with the base line by a reversed curve and right-angled notch. Immediately above the upper line and following the curve are the words "United States of America." Above this is a border line, the middle third of which swells upward, and on this is the device "Commemorative series, 1901", not in panel, but following the upper line. On either side of the opening is a dolphin, head down, and outside this a trident pointing up and the middle prong passing through the scroll end of a tablet. The legend is on a panel with rounded ends, and both it and the words of denomination at the bottom are in straight lines.

These stamps were first placed on sale May 1, 1901, at Buffalo, N. Y.

ORDINARY POSTAGE STAMPS—ISSUE OF 1902–3

This series of postage stamps, known as the 1902 series, was issued to replace the series of 1894. After the new 2-cent stamp was issued it was decided that a more artistic design could be made, and the Bureau of Engraving and Printing was requested to prepare one. This improved design was first issued to postmasters November 12, 1903.

To add historical and educational interest to the series, the name of the person whose portrait is presented appears on each stamp, and the years of birth and death. The words "Series 1902" appear in small type upon each of the stamps, with the legend "United States of America", "Postage", and the denomination in words in bold-faced white letters as well as in Arabic numerals. Briefly, the series is made up as follows:

Denomination	Subject	Color	Issued
1-cent	Franklin	Green	Feb. 3, 1903
2-cent	Washington	Red	Jan. 17, 1903
2-cent (revised design)	Washington	Red	Nov. 12, 1903
3-cent	Jackson	Purple	Feb. 11, 1903
4-cent	Grant	Brown	Feb. 10, 1903
5-cent	Lincoln	Blue	Jan. 20, 1903
6-cent	Garfield	Magenta	Feb. 20, 1903
8-cent	Martha Washington	Dark lilac	Dec. 6, 1902
10-cent	Webster	Light brown	Feb. 5, 1903
10-cent (special delivery)	Boy on bicycle	Light blue	Dec. 9, 1902
13-cent	Harrison	Dark slate	Nov. 18, 1902
15-cent	Clay	Olive	May 27, 1903
50-cent	Jefferson	Orange	Mar. 23, 1903
$1	Farragut	Black	June 5, 1903
$2	Madison	Steel blue	June 5, 1903
$5	Marshall	Dark green	June 5, 1903

FURTHER DESCRIPTION OF THE 1902-3 SERIES

One-cent.—Portrait of Franklin, on each side of which is a child's figure, nude, except for flowing drapery about the loins, holding aloft in the upper corners of the stamp an electric-light bulb.

Two-cent.—The portrait of Washington, by Stuart, is in an elliptical opening $\frac{9}{16}$ of an inch axis, on each side of which a United States flag falls; the Arabic numeral "2" appears in the lower corners in scroll and leaf surroundings.

Two-cent (revised design).—The Stuart portrait of Washington is employed as the subject, but the head is larger than in the first 2-cent stamp of the 1902 series. The opening is an oblong on end, the top line curving upward; the background is a United States shield; the numeral "2" on the lower left side of the portrait is surrounded by a laurel wreath; that on the right side by an oak wreath.

Three-cent.—The portrait of Jackson, whose shoulders are cloaked, has on each side the upper half a bearded man with naked front. The waist is encircled by a belt with a shield-shaped buckle. One arm is bent above the head and the other forearm flexed upward from the elbow, the hands supporting a robe over the head, back, and sides. The portrait opening is formed by the sides of these figures, and the numerals of value cover the lower limbs of the figure; an arched line above and a straight horizontal line below.

Four-cent.—Portrait of Grant. The distinctive features of the border are eagles' heads looking outward in the upper corners, with a well-defined arch, including perpendicular haunches extending slightly below the half circle, as the inclosing line of the portrait. Wreaths of oak leaves surround the numerals near the lower corners, and above each of these numerals are two small flags whose staffs lean outward.

Five-cent.—Portrait of Lincoln. Female figures full robed, except the arms, are resting against the portrait line, and crossing wands of palm over the vignette, with flags floating behind their heads. The numerals are in the lower corners.

Six-cent.—Portrait of Garfield. The border of this stamp is architectural, consisting, as a main feature, of a fluted pilaster on each side, midway of which is a fancy tablet bearing the numeral "6."

Eight-cent.—Martha Washington. The vignette-inclosing line, bearing the words "United States of America" on the upper half, is bordered by a laurel wreath on the sides, leaving an unconnected space above, which is filled with the words "Series 1902." The face is after the painting by Stuart.

Ten-cent.—Portrait of Webster. The ornamental frame consists principally of lateral fasces with battle-axes projecting from their tops, edges outward.

Ten-cent (special delivery).—At each side is a fluted pillar supporting a tablet upon which are the words "United States of America." A messenger boy riding a bicycle toward the right appears on the left end, and the words "Special delivery," "Secures immediate delivery at any United States post office," are across the face of the stamp. The numerals "10" are in the lower corners in foliated spaces.

Thirteen-cent.—Portrait of Harrison. Resting on each side of the upper half of the elliptical opening for the portrait is a seminude female figure, the lower limbs being draped. That on the right holds a mallet in her right hand, while the left rests on a carved head. That on the left supports with her right hand a book resting on her knee, and the left pushes back the mantle covering her head. The bases supporting these figures and partly hidden columns carry the numerals "13."

Fifteen-cent.—Portrait of Clay. The border consists essentially of portions of an oak wreath showing on the sides, and outside of that appears a short bead line on each side curved with the wreath.

Fifty-cent.—Portrait of Jefferson. The upper corners between the frame of the stamp and the ellipse (which is broken at the bottom by a straight horizontal line) surrounding the vignette are filled by foliate ornaments. Perched eagles with their beaks outward fill the lower corners; upon these are placed the denomination numerals "50." The original painting of Jefferson is by Gilbert Stuart.

One-dollar.—Portrait of Farragut. The superior border line of the portrait is a half circle. The denomination numerals and the dollar sign appear in the upper corners. A marine holding a musket sits in the lower left-hand corner and a sailor supporting a boat hook in the right.

Two-dollar.—Portrait of Madison, after the painting by Gilbert Stuart, looking from a circular opening. The border is noticeable from the sprays of palm on the sides, the stems extending behind and below a sharp-pointed shield on each lower corner, upon which the denomination in an Arabic numeral is placed.

Five-dollar.—Portrait of Marshall. The vignette is inclosed above by a line describing a half ellipse cut through its lower minor axis. Architectural design predominates in the border; fluted columns form the sides, and on either end of the entablature, immediately above the pillars upon which it rests, are the mythological heads of Liberty and Justice facing each other on the left and right, respectively. The numerals are on scrolled backgrounds near the lower corners.

LOUISIANA PURCHASE COMMEMORATIVE STAMPS—ISSUE OF 1904

Beginning April 21, a series of postage stamps to commemorate the Louisiana purchase was issued for sale during the term of the Louisiana Purchase Exposition, from May 1 to December 1, 1904.

This series is as follows:

Denomination	Color	Subject
1-cent	Green	Robert R. Livingston.
2-cent	Red	Thomas Jefferson.
3-cent	Purple	James Monroe.
5-cent	Blue	William McKinley.
10-cent	Brown	Map showing territory of Louisiana purchase.

The size of the 1904 commemorative stamp is $\frac{31}{32}$ by $1\frac{3}{8}$ inches; the words "Commemorative series of 1904" in small type appear at the top of each design, with the legend "United States of America" in prominent type; and the surnames of the subjects of the 1-, 2-, 3-, and 5-cent denominations, with years of birth and death, also the denominations spelled out, are shown in the lower portion.

The purpose was to make the subjects of this series of stamps appropriate. Thus Livingston, who as United States minister to France conducted the negotiations for the Louisiana purchase; Jefferson, President of the United States at the time of the purchase; Monroe, special ambassador to France in the matter of the purchase, who with Livingston closed the negotiations; McKinley, who as President, approved the acts of Congress officially connecting the Government with the commemorative exposition; and the 10-cent stamp showing the territory of the purchase itself.

Following is a description in some detail of the several denominations:

One-cent.—On either side of Livingston's portrait are fluted pillars supporting a plain arch; landscapes are on either side of the portrait, the one on the left representing the swamp country of the extreme south of the purchase, that on the right an immigrant wagon approaching the mountains in the extreme northwest; in the lower corners are shields surrounding the numeral "1"; a ribbon under the portrait bears the name and the years of birth and death of the subject; a panel along the base contains the words "Postage, one cent."

Two-cent.—Over the portrait of Jefferson is a flat arch support by fluted columns; the numeral "2" on either side is surrounded by an ellipse on end within laurel wreaths, and underneath the wreaths are ribbons showing years of birth and death of the subject; the name "Jefferson" appears in a scroll under the portrait; a panel at the base of the stamp bears the words "Postage, two cents."

Three-cent.—Below the portrait of Monroe is a ribbon showing his name, with years of birth and death. The portrait is partly surrounded by a wreath of laurel; on either side are ornamental shields exhibiting the numeral "3"; the portrait, wreath, and ribbon are within an ornamental panel; the words "Postage, three cents" appear along the lower part of the stamp.

Five-cent.—The face of the stamp is divided into three panels by Corinthian columns supporting a panel at the top, in which the words "United States of America" appear. The portrait of McKinley is within a circle in the center panel, with the numeral "5" in an ornamental shield on either side. At the base of the panels are two palm branches separating the panels from the wording "Postage, five cents." Beneath the portrait is a ribbon bearing the name and years of birth and death of the subject.

Ten-cent.—The central figure is a map of the United States, showing the territory of the Louisiana purchase in dark tint, with the year of the purchase, "1803", obliquely across the face of the shaded portion; the border is composed of a column at either end, with ornamental shields at the bases bearing the numeral "10"; panels along the top and bottom contain the lettering.

These stamps were first placed on sale April 21, 1904, at New Orleans, La.

JAMESTOWN COMMEMORATIVE STAMPS—ISSUE OF 1907

A new series of postage stamps to commemorate the founding of Jamestown, the tercentennial of which was celebrated during 1907, was issued beginning April 25, 1907. The stamps are described as follows:

Denomination	Color	Subject
1-cent	Green	Capt. John Smith.
2-cent	Red	Founding of Jamestown.
5-cent	Blue	Pocahontas.

The stamps are rectangular in shape, $^{49}\!/_{64}$ by $1^{3}\!/_{64}$ inches in size, and of three denominations, 1-cent green, 2-cent red, and 5-cent blue.

The 1-cent contains, in a semicircular frame, the portrait of Capt. John Smith, taken from an old engraving. In the upper corners are medallions in relief, in oval frames, of Pocahontas and Powhatan; in the lower corners, shields with the numeral "1"; upon a scroll surrounding the portrait and conforming to the semicircle is the legend, "Founding of Jamestown, 1607"; on the base, "Captain John Smith", with the years of his birth and death, 1580–1631. In the semicircle above the head are the words "United States of America"; across the extreme top and bottom, in white letters in green panels, are the words, "Commemorative series, 1907", and "Postage, one cent."

The 2-cent stamp contains a picture depicting the landing of the adventurers at Jamestown in 1607. On one side is a tobacco plant, and on the other a stalk of Indian corn. Underneath, on a scroll, are the words, "Founding of Jamestown, 1607." In a curved panel over the picture, in white letters, are the words "United States of America"; on the extreme top and bottom, in white letters on red background, "Commemorative series, 1907", and the words "Postage, two cents." In each lower corner is a shield with the numeral "2."

The 5-cent stamp contains a portrait, in an oval frame, of Pocahontas. In a panel at the top, in white letters, are the words "United States of America." At the bottom, in a panel, are the words "Postage, five cents"; under the portrait, on a scroll, "Pocahontas", and the years of birth and death, 1595–1617. On either side of the portrait are shields, their bases resting on the lower panel, containing the numeral "5." Arising from behind these shields are scrolls with the words, "Founding of Jamestown, 1607." In vertical panels on the right and left are the words "Commemorative series, 1907."

The 1-cent and 2-cent denominations were first placed on sale April 25, 1907, at Jamestown, Va., and the 5-cent stamp at the same post office on May 3, 1907.

ORDINARY POSTAGE STAMPS—ISSUE OF 1908-9

This series of postage stamps was issued to replace the regular issue of adhesive stamps, known as the "Series of 1902." Description follows:

Denomination	Color	Subject	Issued
1-cent	Green	Franklin	Dec. 2, 1908
2-cent	Red	Washington	Nov. 16, 1908
3-cent	Purple	Washington	Dec. 24, 1908
4-cent	Brown	Washington	Dec. 24, 1908
5-cent	Dark blue	Washington	Dec. 19, 1008
6-cent	Orange	Washington	Dec. 31, 1908
8-cent	Olive	Washington	Dec. 12, 1908
10-cent	Yellow	Washington	Jan. 7, 1909
10-cent special-delivery	Green	Winged hat of Mercury and olive branch	Dec. 12, 1908
13-cent	Sea green	Washington	Jan. 11, 1909
15-cent	Light blue	Washington	Jan. 19, 1909
50-cent	Lavender	Washington	Jan. 13, 1909
$1	Dark slate	Washington	Jan. 29, 1909

For the sake of uniformity and artistic effect, the head of Washington (a profile from Houdon's bust) was adopted as the subject of all the denominations except the 1-cent, which bears the head of Franklin (the first Postmaster General). The border designs are identical on all the stamps, the head appearing within an ellipse on end, with laurel leaves on either side of the ellipse. Above the head are the words "U. S. postage"; below it, the denomination expressed *in words on the 1-cent* and *2-cent* and in *numerals on the other denominations.*

The $2 and $5 denominations are not represented in this series, as there was little need for these high denominations since the reduction of rates of letter postage to certain foreign countries and the increase in the unit weight of international postage.

A marked departure was made in the special-delivery stamp of the series of 1908. The design was artistic, but many complaints were received from the public and from postmasters that letters bearing the new stamp were escaping special-delivery treatment on account of the altered shape, design, and *color.*

It was finally decided to discontinue this stamp, and this was done by order of the Postmaster General dated June 9, 1909, and the issuance of the special-delivery stamp of the 1902 series was resumed.

The green special-delivery stamp, issue of 1908, is described as follows:

Size, $84/100$ by $11/100$ inches; color, green. In the upper left corner is the denomination "10" in figures inclosed within a circle. Running diagonally from the lower left corner appears an olive branch entwining the winged hat of Mercury. In the lower right-hand portion of the stamp is the inscription "U. S. postage, special delivery", in a rectangular panel.

The number of green special-delivery stamps of the 1908 series issued was 3,876,551.

LINCOLN MEMORIAL STAMP (2-CENT)—ISSUE OF 1909

On January 22, 1909, Congress adopted a joint resolution reading:

"Resolved by the Senate and House of Representatives of the United States of America in Congress assembled, That the Postmaster General is hereby authorized to design and issue a special postage stamp, of the denomination of 2 cents, in commemoration of the one-hundredth anniversary of the birth of Abraham Lincoln."

Under this resolution a postage stamp was prepared and issued to postmasters in time for sale to the public beginning on Lincoln's birthday, February 12. This stamp is described as follows:

Size and shape, the same as of the regular issue of postage stamps; color, red. The subject is a profile, within an ellipse on end, of the head of Lincoln from St. Gaudens's statue. A spray of laurel leaves appears on either side of the ellipse. Above the subject appear the words "U. S. postage." Below, the ellipse is broken by a ribbon containing the dates of Lincoln's birth and the one-hundredth anniversary thereof (1809—February 12—1909), with the denomination in words (two cents) beneath.

ALASKA-YUKON-PACIFIC STAMP (2-CENT)—ISSUE OF 1909

To commemorate the development of the Alaska-Yukon-Pacific Territory, which was celebrated by an exposition at Seattle, Wash., in 1909, the department issued a postage stamp of special design, which was first placed on sale June 1, 1909, at Seattle, Wash.

The stamp is $^{49}/_{64}$ by $1^{3}/_{64}$ inches in dimension, arranged horizontally, and is printed in red ink. At the top and bottom are panels containing, respectively, the words "U. S. postage" and "Two cents." In the center the larger part of a circle rests on the lower panel and incloses a ribbon bearing the words "Alaska-Yukon-Pacific 1909", and in the center of the circle appears a portrait of William H. Seward, who as Secretary of State conducted the negotiations for the purchase of Alaska from Russia. The name "William H. Seward" appears under the portrait. On either side is an ellipse containing the Arabic numeral "2" with laurel branches as a background.

HUDSON-FULTON STAMP (2-CENT)—ISSUE OF 1909

The tercentenary of the discovery of the Hudson River and the centennial of its first navigation by steam, which was celebrated in 1909, was also commemorated with a special postage stamp, which was first placed on sale September 25, 1909, at New York, N. Y.

The stamp is about $^{7}/_{8}$ by $1^{3}/_{8}$ inches in dimension, arranged horizontally, and printed in red ink. At the top appears the inscription "Hudson-Fulton Celebration", with the years "1609" and "1909" immediately thereunder on either side. Below this inscription in a curved line are the words "U. S. postage." At the bottom on each side is a prominent Arabic numeral "2", with the words "Two cents" in a panel between the figures. In the center is engraved a picture showing the Palisades of the Hudson River in the background, with the *Half Moon* sailing up the river and the *Clermont* steaming in the opposite direction. In the foreground is an Indian in a canoe, and in the distance, just discernible, is a canoe containing four other Indians, the canoes representing the first means of navigating the river.

POSTAL SAVINGS OFFICIAL STAMPS—ISSUE OF 1911

The act of Congress approved June 25, 1910, establishing postal savings depositories, provides:

"SEC. 2. That the Postmaster General is hereby directed to prepare and issue special stamps of the necessary denominations for use, in lieu of penalty or franked envelopes, in the transmittal of free mail resulting from the administration of this act."

Under this provision of law the department issued postal savings official stamps in five denominations, described as follows:

Denomination	Color	Issued
1-cent	Purple	Mar. 27, 1911
2-cent	Black	Dec. 22, 1910
10-cent	Red	Feb. 1, 1911
50-cent	Green	Feb. 1, 1911
$1	Blue	Feb. 1, 1911

The stamp is a rectangle on end, of about the same size as an ordinary postage stamp. In the center is an ellipse containing the words "Official mail" in white letters, the background within the ellipse being lathe work. Outside of and following the curve of the ellipse are the words "U. S. postal savings" in white letters. In each lower corner is a numeral expressing the denomination, and between these numerals the word "Cents" (or "Dollar") appears in white letters. In the corners at the top are small triangular panels containing relief work.

There was also issued a 1-cent and 2-cent official stamped envelope for use of the postal savings. The embossed stamp is an ellipse on end; in the center in plain gothic type appear the words "Official mail" in two horizontal lines. In the upper half of the border are the words "U. S. postal savings", and in the lower half "One 1 cent" (or "Two 2 cents"), the numerals being prominent.

The use of postal savings official stamps was discontinued by the act of Congress approved September 23, 1914, providing the penalty privilege for official business of the Postal Savings System.

The unused stamps in the hands of postmasters were returned to the department and later destroyed by a committee appointed for that purpose.

REGISTRY STAMP (10-CENT)—ISSUE OF 1911

This stamp, of 10-cent denomination, was originated by the Postmaster General to prepay registry fees. It is of special design, in order to identify mail to which it is attached as registered matter and entitled to all the benefits and safeguards of the system. A description follows:

The registry stamp is a rectangle on end; the size of the design is approximately ¾ by ⅞ inch; the color is light blue. The design shows an eagle with extended wings, perched upon a rock, within a circle set in a panel of plain lines. Above the circle and following its curve the words "United States registry" appear in two lines; and in the two lower corners the denomination "10" appears within small circles, with the word "Cents" between.

A supply of the registry stamps was placed on sale in post offices December 1, 1911, in time for use in connection with holiday mailings.

It was later found that the slight advantage of the distinctive registry stamp was outweighed by the confusion arising from its attempted use for prepayment of postage by persons unfamiliar with its true function. Moreover, ordinary stamps are valid for payment of registry fees, so that the registry stamp is not essential. Such a stamp is not required by law; it was issued by Executive order.

The Postmaster General, in Order No. 7136, dated May 28, 1913, directed the discontinuance of the issuance of the registry stamps when the manufactured supply on hand shall have become exhausted. They will continue, however, to be valid for registry fees so long as any of the stamps remain unused.

ORDINARY POSTAGE STAMPS—ISSUE OF 1912

CHANGES IN DESIGN AND COLOR

The postage stamps of the 1908 issue, while possessing high artistic merit, have given considerable trouble to the public and to the Postal Service on account of the similarity of designs of the different denominations. All of the 12 stamps are of identical design, except that the 1-cent denomination bears the portrait of Franklin, while the others bear the portrait of Washington. There was not a sufficient number of distinctive colors for all the stamps, making it necessary above the 6-cent to use different shades of the same colors given the lower denominations. Thus, the 1-cent and 8-cent are different shades of green; the 3-cent and 50-cent are different shades of purple; the 5-cent and 15-cent are different shades of blue. In the rapid handling of mail matter one denomination was very apt to be mistaken for another, particularly under artificial light. The first six stamps are of sufficiently contrasting colors, but it was decided to change the subject of the 1-cent from Franklin to Washington and to change the 1-cent and 2-cent so as to express the denomination in numerals instead of in words, thus conforming to the other stamps of the series. No change was made in the 3-, 4-, 5-, or 6-cent stamps from those of the 1908 issue, but to give more marked contrast to the remaining five denominations (the 13-cent stamp having been discontinued) a change was made in the border design. The stamps of the 1912 issue combine utility with art and harmony, presenting the head of the first President on the first six denominations and that of the first Postmaster General, with a different border design, on the last five. Descriptions follow:

Denomination	Color	Subject	Issued
1-cent	Green	Washington	Feb. 12, 1912
2-cent	Red	Washington	Feb. 12, 1912
3-cent	Purple	Washington	(1)
4-cent	Brown	Washington	(1)
5-cent	Dark blue	Washington	(1)
6-cent	Orange	Washington	(1)
8-cent	Olive	Franklin	Feb. 12, 1912
10-cent	Dark yellow	Franklin	Jan. 11, 1912
15-cent	Gray	Franklin	Feb. 12, 1912
50-cent	Lavender	Franklin	Feb. 12, 1912
$1	Dark brown	Franklin	Feb. 12, 1912

[1] Same as 1908 issue.

The 1-, 2-, 3-, 4-, 5-, and 6-cent stamps bear the head of Washington in profile, from Houdon's bust, looking to the left. The borders of the first six denominations are identical, and of the same design as the series of 1908. The portrait of Washington appears within a plain ellipse on end, with branches of laurel on either side. Above the head in a straight line are the words "U. S. postage"; in capital letters below it the word "Cents", with the denomination in numerals in both lower corners.

The colors of the five higher denominations are: 8-cent, olive; 10-cent, dark yellow; 15-cent, gray; 50-cent, lavender; $1, dark brown. The subject of these stamps is a portrait of Franklin in profile, from Houdon's bust, looking to the left, within an ellipse on end. In the upper corners are plain panels in the form of right angles; above the ellipse and following it in a curved line are the words "U. S. postage" in capital letters; on either side of the lower part of the ellipse are branches of oak leaves; in the two lower corners the denomination appears in numerals, and between them is the word "Cents" (or "Dollar") in a horizontal panel which breaks the base of the ellipse.

The department's supply of 13-cent stamps became exhausted and the denomination was discontinued, its primary purpose to prepay postage and registry fee on foreign mailings having ceased to exist when the registry fee was increased to 10 cents.

PANAMA-PACIFIC COMMEMORATIVE STAMP—ISSUE OF 1913

This series of postage stamps, issued to commemorate the opening of the Panama Canal and the discovery of the Pacific Ocean, comprises four denominations, 1, 2, 5, and 10 cents, all of which were first placed on sale at San Francisco, Calif., January 1, 1913, except the 2-cent denomination, which was first placed on sale at the same post office on January 18, 1913. Description follows:

Denomination	Color	Subject
1-cent	Green	Balboa, 1513.
2-cent	Carmine	Panama Canal.
5-cent	Blue	Golden Gate.
10-cent	Orange	Discovery of San Francisco Bay.

The stamps are about ¾ of an inch high by 1¹⁄₁₆ inches wide; at the top appear the words "U. S. postage" and "San Francisco, 1915"; in the left-hand border is a branch of laurel and in the right-hand border a palm branch; a numeral expressing the denomination is shown within a circle in each lower corner, with the word "Cents" between.

The 1-cent stamp is green and in the center appears, within a circle, a bust of Balboa, discoverer of the Pacific Ocean, looking to the left, and wearing a cuirass and a helmet with a plume. On each side of the background are palm trees, with the ocean in the foreground. Below the portrait, in a horizontal panel breaking the circle, are the words "Balboa, 1513."

The 2-cent stamp is carmine. It represents the Panama Canal, with a merchant steamer emerging from one lock and a warship in the other. The mountains of the Isthmus in the distance, and palm trees on the right-hand side of the locks. Beneath the picture are the words "Panama Canal."

The 5-cent stamp is blue, and presents the Golden Gate of San Francisco Harbor, with the setting sun in the background and a steamer and sailing vessel in the bay. The words "Golden Gate" appear below the picture.

The 10-cent stamp is dark yellow. The subject is "Discovery of San Francisco Bay", from a painting which represents the discovering party looking out upon the distant bay.

A model of the Pedro Miguel Locks was used as the subject of the 2-cent denomination, and the title was first erroneously engraved "Gatun Locks", but the mistake was discovered before any of the stamps were issued, and all of those which had been printed were destroyed by burning. The title was reengraved as "Panama Canal", and the stamps were issued with that title.

The first print of the 10-cent denomination was found to be of too light a shade, and in response to a request of the department, dated April 9, 1913, the Bureau of Engraving and Printing adopted a darker shade of ink. These darker stamps were first issued by the department August 25, 1913.

PARCEL-POST STAMPS—ISSUE OF 1912-13

The act of Congress approved August 24, 1912, making appropriations for the Postal Service for the fiscal year 1913, contains the following provisions as to parcel-post stamps:

"That the rate of postage on fourth-class matter weighing not more than 4 ounces shall be 1 cent for each ounce or fraction of an ounce; and on such matter in excess of 4 ounces in weight the rate shall be by the pound, as hereinafter provided, the postage in all cases to be prepaid by distinctive postage stamps affixed.

"Parcel-post equipment, 1913.—That the Postmaster General shall provide such special equipment, maps, stamps, directories, and printed instructions as may be necessary for the administration of this section * * *."

Under this provision of law the department prepared a set of 12 parcel-post stamps and a set of 5 parcel-post due stamps of distinctive designs. The designs were prepared in 3 groups of 4 stamps each, the working personnel of the Postal Service being represented by the first group, the transportation of the mail by the second group, and the manufacturing and agricultural interests of the country by the third group. Descriptions, with dates of issue of the several denominations, follow:

Denomination	Color	Subject	Date of issue
1-cent	Red	Post-office clerk	Nov. 27, 1912
2-cent	Red	City carrier	Nov. 27, 1912
3-cent	Red	Railway postal clerk	Apr. 5, 1913
4-cent	Red	Rural carrier	Dec. 12, 1912
5-cent	Red	Mail train	Nov. 27, 1912
10-cent	Red	Steamship and mail tender	Dec. 9, 1912
15-cent	Red	Automobile service	Dec. 16, 1912
20-cent	Red	Aeroplane carrying mail	Dec. 16, 1912
25-cent	Red	Manufacturing	Nov. 27, 1912
50-cent	Red	Dairying	Mar. 15, 1913
75-cent	Red	Harvesting	Dec. 18, 1912
$1	Red	Fruit growing	Jan. 3, 1913

The parcel-post stamps are $^{875}\!/_{1000}$ by $1^{375}\!/_{1000}$ inches in dimension. The color is red for all denominations. In a curved panel across the top, supported by a paneled perpendicular column at each end, appear the words "U. S. parcel post" in Roman capital letters. Triangular ornaments occupy both upper corners. The denomination in large numerals is in each lower corner, with the title of the subject and the word "Cents" (or "Dollar") between.

These stamps were first placed on sale January 1, 1913, with the inauguration of the parcel-post law.

PARCEL-POST POSTAGE-DUE STAMPS

The parcel-post postage-due stamps are of the same size as the parcel-post postage stamps. The color is green for all denominations. In a horizontal panel across the top are the words "U. S. parcel post" and, in a similar panel at the bottom, "Postage due", in Roman capital letters. In the center, upon a background of lathework, and within a circular frame, is a larger numeral expressing the denomination. The upper half of the circular frame carries the denomination in words which are repeated in the lower half, except that the words expressing the denomination appear but once upon the 25-cent stamp. Small numerals of denomination are on both sides of the large central numeral. The denominations with dates of issue follow:

Denomination	Color	Date of issue
1-cent	Green	Nov. 27, 1912
2-cent	Green	Dec. 9, 1912
5-cent	Green	Nov. 27, 1912
10-cent	Green	Dec. 12, 1912
25-cent	Green	Dec. 16, 1912

While the parcel-post stamps were of appropriate design and sufficiently distinctive to identify at a glance mail to which they were affixed as parcel-post matter, objections to them began to develop from the outset. All denominations being printed in the same color caused difficulty in handling which the large numerals failed to prevent. Another objection was the size of the stamps, which was too large for small parcels and labels, particularly when more than one stamp was required for postage. The issuing of the stamps in sheets of 45, made necessary by the size of the stamps, was troublesome to the department, to postmasters and their employees, and to the public, because of the difficulty experienced in counting and computing multiples of 45 as compared with the sheets of 100, to which the Postal Service and the public are accustomed.

The objections to the stamps led to steps to reduce the size and change the designs and color scheme. March 21, 1913, the Postmaster General approved a design for a new parcel-post stamp, which was of the same size and shape as the ordinary postage stamp but with the long dimension horizontal instead of vertical, and having a large numeral expressing the denomination in the center in place of the usual picture. The colors were to correspond with those of the ordinary stamps of similar denominations.

No stamps of the new design were printed, however, as the department decided that the distinctive parcel-post stamps could be discontinued entirely. These stamps served but one useful purpose; that is, to indicate the parcel-post revenue, and this object, it was held, could be accomplished with sufficient accuracy for all practical purposes by other means. The distinctive stamps were expensive to produce, handle and account for, and were a source of serious embarrassment and vexation to the public as well as to the Postal Service. These disadvantages far outweighed the single advantage possessed by the stamps as a medium of revenue statistics. The ordinary stamp should be sufficiently elastic for every postage purpose (except payment of postage due) so that it can be used for prepayment of postage on all classes of mail, special-delivery service, and registry, insurance, and C. O. D. fees. Such a broad usefulness saves the public and the Postal Service the inconvenience and annoyance involved in the restricted validity of special stamps, and simplifies and facilitates public patronage of the service.

The parcel-post law provided for the use of distinctive stamps on fourth-class mail, but it also authorized the Postmaster General, with the consent of the Interstate Commerce Commission, to reform the conditions of mailability for the purpose of promoting the service to the public. Under this latter provision, the Postmaster General, with the approval of the Interstate Commerce Commission, in Order No. 7241 of June 26, 1913, effective July 1, 1913, directed that ordinary postage stamps should be valid for postage, insurance, and C. O. D. fees on parcels, and that distinctive parcel-post stamps should be valid for all purposes for which ordinary stamps are valid; also, that the regular issue of due stamps and the distinctive parcel-post due stamps should be valid for the collection of unpaid and short-paid postage on all classes of mail.

It was further ordered that the issuance of distinctive parcel-post stamps and parcel-post due stamps be discontinued after the existing stocks were exhausted and that no additional supplies should be printed.

ORDINARY POSTAGE STAMPS—ISSUE OF 1914

NEW DENOMINATIONS

The discontinuance of distinctive parcel-post stamps made it necessary to issue five new denominations of ordinary stamps to take their place. The new stamps are of the same shape (a rectangle on end) and size (about ⅞ by ³³⁄₃₂ inch) as the other ordinary stamps, series of 1912, and are described as follows:

Denomination	Color	Subject	Date of issue
7-cent	Black	Washington	Apr. 29, 1914
9-cent	Pink	Franklin	Apr. 29, 1914
12-cent	Maroon	Franklin	Apr. 29, 1914
20-cent	Light blue	Franklin	Apr. 29, 1914
30-cent	Orange-red	Franklin	Apr. 29, 1914

The 7-cent stamp bears the head of Washington in profile, from Houdon's bust, looking to the left. The border design is the same as that of the first six denominations of the current series.

The 9-cent, 12-cent, 20-cent, and 30-cent stamps bear the head of Franklin in profile, from Houdon's bust, looking to the left. These four denominations have the same border design as the current 8-cent to $1 stamps.

In addition to its use on parcels, the new 12-cent stamp was convenient for prepayment of registration or special-delivery fee with a single rate of letter postage.

ORDINARY POSTAGE STAMP (11-CENT)—ISSUE OF 1915

NEW DENOMINATION

A new postage stamp of 11-cent denomination was issued August 9, 1915; it bears the head of Franklin in profile, from Houdon's bust, looking to the left, and is printed in dark green ink. It is of the same shape (a rectangle on end) and size (about ⅞ by ²³⁄₃₂ inch) as the other ordinary stamps, series of 1912. The border design is the same as that of the other denominations of the current issue above 7 cents. This new stamp was issued primarily for use in prepaying postage on parcels, and postage and insurance fee on insured parcels, amounting to 11 cents, and it makes the series of denominations complete from 1 cent to 12 cents.

AIR-MAIL STAMPS—ISSUE OF 1918

Denomination	Color	Subject
6-cent	Orange	Mail airplane.
16-cent	Green	Mail airplane.
24-cent	Red and blue	Mail airplane.

Air-mail service was established May 15, 1918, between Washington, Philadelphia, and New York. Letters and sealed parcels, the latter not exceeding 30 inches in length and girth combined, could be mailed at Washington, Philadelphia, and New York for any city in the United States or its possessions.

The rate of postage was fixed at 24 cents per ounce or fraction thereof, which included special-delivery service.

To meet this postage requirement, the department issued a distinctive stamp in the 24-cent denomination, which was first placed on sale May 13, 1918, at Washington, D. C.

The stamp is rectangular in shape, about ⅞ inch long and ¾ inch high. The central design is a mail airplane in flight. Above, in a curved line of Roman capital letters, are the words "U. S. postage." Triangular ornaments appear in the two upper corners. Below the airplane, in a straight line of Roman capital letters, is the word "Cents", with the numerals "24" within circles in the two lower corners. The stamp is printed in two colors; the border design is red and the airplane is blue.

The rate of postage for air-mail service was changed to 16 cents, effective July 15, 1918, and the department issued a new air-mail postage stamp of the 16-cent denomination, which was first placed on sale July 11, 1918, at Washington, D. C. The design is the same as the 24-cent stamp, except that the numerals "16" appear within the circles in the two lower corners and the color is green.

The rate of postage on air-mail matter was reduced to 6 cents, effective December 15, 1918. This rate did not include special-delivery service.

A new air-mail stamp of the 6-cent denomination was issued to conform to the new rate, but no change was made in the design of this stamp from that of the 16-cent and 24-cent air-mail stamps, except that the numeral "6" appears within the circles in the two lower corners and the color is orange. This stamp was first placed on sale at Washington, D. C., on December 10, 1918.

ORDINARY POSTAGE STAMPS—ISSUE OF 1918

The department issued on August 19, 1918, a $2 and $5 postage stamp of new design, printed in two colors. A description of the $2 stamp follows:

The stamp is rectangular in shape, about ⅞ inch wide and ¾ inch high. The subject is a portrait of Franklin looking to the left, printed in black ink. The border design is red. Triangular ornaments appear in the two upper corners, and the words "U. S. postage" are printed in Roman capital letters in a curved line above the head of Franklin. The word "Dollars" is printed in a straight line of Roman capital letters below the portrait, and the numeral "2" appears within ovals in both lower corners.

The design of the $5 stamp is the same as the $2 except that it bears the numeral "5" in the lower corners, and the border is printed in green ink with the head of Franklin in black.

ORDINARY POSTAGE STAMP (13-CENT)—ISSUE OF 1919

NEW DENOMINATION

A new postage stamp of 13-cent denomination was issued January 10, 1919, and is described as follows:

This stamp bears the head of Franklin in profile, from Houdon's bust, looking to the left, and is printed in light green ink. It is of the same shape (a rectangle on end) and size (about ⅞ by ¾ inch) as the other ordinary stamps, series of 1912. The border design is the same as that of the other denominations of the current issue above 7-cent.

The new stamp was issued primarily for use in prepaying a single rate of letter postage and special-delivery fee, or for postage and registry fee, and was also available to the amount of its value for other purposes for which ordinary postage stamps are used.

VICTORY STAMP (3-CENT)—ISSUE OF 1919

A Victory postage stamp of 3-cent denomination was issued March 3, 1919, to commemorate the successful outcome of the World War.

The stamp is $^{27}\!/_{32}$ by ¾ inch in dimension, arranged horizontally, and is printed in purple. The design presents a standing figure of Liberty Victorious, with a background composed of the flags of the five countries which were most actively engaged in the cause.

The figure of Liberty is helmeted, the upper part of the body is encased in scale armor, and a flowing skirt falls to the feet. The right hand grasps a sword, the point of which rests on the ground at the feet of the figure; the left arm is partially extended, and the hand holds a balance scale representing justice.

Back of the figure appears the American flag; at the left are draped the British and Belgian flags, and at the right the Italian and French flags.

The whole design appears upon a shaded panel. Extending across the top, in a straight line of Roman capital letters, is the inscription "U. S. postage." At the bottom, directly beneath the figure, in a straight line of Roman capitals, is the word "Cents" flanked by circles containing the numeral "3" in each lower corner of the stamp. This stamp was first placed on sale March 3, 1919, at Washington, D. C.

ORDINARY POSTAGE STAMPS (SURCHARGED "SHANGHAI, CHINA")—ISSUE OF 1919

Postage stamps of the current series were issued to the United States postal agency, Shanghai, China, in denominations of 1-, 2-, 3-, 4-, 5-, 6-, 7-, 8-, 9-, 10-, 12-, 15-, 20-, 30-, 50-cent and $1; surcharged "Shanghai, China", at double the original value of the stamps; that is to say, the 1-cent stamp is surcharged 2 cents, the 2-cent stamp is surcharged 4 cents, and so on through the list. The surcharge is printed in black letters on all denominations except 7-cent and $1, which are surcharged with red ink. For example, the 1-cent stamp is surcharged as follows:

SHANGHAI

2¢

CHINA

Owing to the small demand for 10-cent special-delivery stamps at the United States postal agency, Shanghai, China, no 10-cent special-delivery stamps surcharged "Shanghai, China", were printed.

These stamps were intended for sale by the postal agency at Shanghai at their surcharged value in local currency, and were valid to the amount of their original values for the prepayment of postage on mail dispatched from the United States postal agency at Shanghai to addresses in the United States.

The stamps were first issued May 24, 1919, and were placed on sale at Shanghai, China, July 1, 1919. They were not issued to postmasters in the United States.

PILGRIM TERCENTENARY COMMEMORATIVE STAMPS—ISSUE OF 1920

A special series of postage stamps was issued in commemoration of the tercentenary of the landing of the Pilgrims in December of 1620. These stamps were issued in pursuance of section 4 of Public Resolution No. 42, Sixty-sixth Congress, approved May 13, 1920, providing as follows:

"SEC. 4. That the Postmaster General is hereby authorized and directed to issue a special series of postage stamps, in such denominations and of such design as he may determine, commemorative of the three hundredth anniversary of the landing of the Pilgrims at Provincetown and Plymouth, Massachusetts."

The stamps are in three denominations, described as follows:

Denomination	Color	Subject
1-cent	Green	The Mayflower.
2-cent	Red	Landing of the Pilgrims.
5 cent	Blue	Signing of the compact.

The dimensions of the stamps are approximately ¾ by 1¹⁄₁₆ inches. In a straight horizontal line at the top are the words "Pilgrim Tercentenary"; directly below, at the left and right, are the years "1620" and "1920." Beneath the subject appears its title upon a curving ribbon. Within circles in the two lower corners are numerals of denomination, with the word "Cents" in a straight horizontal line between. The border at the left of the picture presents a vertical row of hawthorn blossoms (the British Mayflower); the border at the right contains a row of trailing arbutus (the American Mayflower, which tradition says was named by the Pilgrims after their ship).

The Pilgrim Tercentenary stamps were issued in sheets of 70 and were first placed on sale Dec. 18, 1920, at Provincetown and Plymouth, Mass.

SPECIAL-DELIVERY STAMP (10-CENT)—ISSUE OF 1922

A special-delivery stamp of new design was issued July 11, 1922, and placed on sale at Washington, D. C., July 12, 1922. The stamp replaced the special-delivery stamp known as the issue of 1902. A description follows:

The stamp is the same shape and size, $14^{2}/_{100}$ by $8^{3}/_{100}$ inch, as the former special-delivery stamp, and is printed in blue ink. The central design is the front of a private residence, showing a motorcycle parked against the curb with the special-delivery messenger delivering a letter. At the top of the stamp in white-face Roman appear the words "United States postage", and in two ribbons just below, and on either side of the picture, appear the words "Special" and "Delivery" in dark letters. To the right, and just above the motorcycle, are the words "At any United States post office", and in both lower corners are circles containing the numerals "10" connected by a panel in which appear the words "Ten cents" in white letters. A simple straight-line border surrounds the stamp.

ORDINARY POSTAGE STAMPS—ISSUE OF 1922–23

This series of postage stamps was issued to replace the regular issue of stamps, known as the "Series of 1912."

There are 21 denominations in this series, each having a different subject as the central design and with larger numerals denoting the denominations.

The designs are most artistic and were selected with the view of giving historical and educational interest to the stamps. Three different border designs were used for this series of stamps, which are the same size, $75/100$ by $87/100$ inch, as the 1912 issue.

The border design for the first 13 denominations (1-cent to 14-cent) is identical. A different border design was used for the 15-cent denomination and still another border design for the remaining seven denominations (20-cent, 25-cent, 30-cent, 50-cent, $1, $2, and $5).

The stamps are described as follows:

Denomination	Color	Subject	Placed on sale
1-cent	Green	Franklin	Jan. 17, 1923
2-cent	Red	Washington	Jan. 15, 1923
3-cent	Purple	Lincoln	Feb. 12, 1923
4-cent	Brown	Martha Washington	Jan. 15, 1923
5-cent	Blue	Roosevelt	Oct. 27, 1922
6-cent	Orange	Garfield	Nov. 20, 1922
7-cent	Black	McKinley	May 1, 1923
8-cent	Olive	Grant	May 1, 1923
9-cent	Pink	Jefferson	Jan. 15, 1923
10-cent:	Yellow	Monroe	Jan. 15, 1923
11-cent	Light blue	Hayes	Oct. 4, 1922
12-cent	Purplish brown	Cleveland	Mar. 20, 1923
14-cent	Indigo	American Indian	May 1, 1923
15-cent	Dark gray	Liberty	Nov. 11, 1922
20-cent	Crimson	Golden Gate	May 1, 1923
25-cent	Dark green	Niagara	Nov. 11, 1922
30-cent	Sepia	Buffalo	Mar. 20, 1923
50-cent	Lavender	Arlington Amphitheatre	Nov. 11, 1922
$1	Brown	Lincoln Memorial	Feb. 12, 1923
$2	Blue	United States Capitol	Mar. 20, 1923
$5	Red and blue	America	Mar. 20, 1923

One-cent.—Portrait of Franklin, from Houdon's bust, within an oval and partly inclosed in a panel which is supported on either side by acanthus scrolls. Above the portrait in a curved line appear the words "United States postage" in white Roman letters. On a ribbon below the oval is the name "Franklin" and under this, at the bottom of the stamp, appears the word "Cent." In both lower corners within ovals with dark backgrounds is the white numeral "1." The entire stamp is inclosed within a cross-line border with small triangular ornaments in both upper corners. Printed in green ink. The 1-cent stamp was first placed on sale at Washington, D. C., and Philadelphia, Pa., on Franklin's birthday, January 17, 1923.

Two-cent.—Portrait of Washington, from Houdon's bust, with the name "Washington" on the ribbon below the portrait. The surrounding design is the same as the 1-cent stamp, with the necessary change of figures representing the denomination, and with the word "Cents" instead of "Cent." The stamp is printed in red ink. The 2-cent stamp was first placed on sale at Washington, D. C., January 15, 1923, in sheet form. This denomination was, however, first issued in coils January 8, 1923, and was placed on sale the following day.

Three-cent.—Portrait of Lincoln, from photograph, with the name "Lincoln" on the ribbon below the portrait. The surrounding design is the same as the 2-cent stamp, with the necessary change of figures representing the denomination. The stamp is printed in purple ink. The 3-cent stamp was first placed on sale at Washington, D. C., and Hodgenville, Larue County, Ky., the birthplace of former President Lincoln, on his birthday, February 12, 1923.

Four-cent.—Portrait of Martha Washington, after painting by Gilbert Stuart, with the name "Martha Washington" on the ribbon below the portrait. The surrounding design is the same as the 2-cent stamp, with the necessary change of numerals representing the denomination. The stamp is printed in brown ink and was placed on sale at Washington, D. C., on January 15, 1923.

Five-cent.—Portrait of Roosevelt, from photograph, with the name "Roosevelt" on the ribbon below the portrait. The surrounding design is the same as the 2-cent stamp, with the necessary change of numerals representing the denomination. The stamp is printed in blue ink. The 5-cent stamp was first placed on sale at Washington, D. C., Oyster Bay, N. Y., and New York, N. Y., October 27, 1922, the birthday of former President Roosevelt.

Six-cent.—Portrait of Garfield, from photograph, with the name "Garfield" on the ribbon below the portrait. The surrounding design is the same as the 2-cent stamp, with the necessary change of numerals representing the denomination. The stamp is printed in orange ink and was placed on sale November 20, 1922, at Washington, D. C.

Seven-cent.—Portrait of McKinley, from photograph, with the name "McKinley" on the ribbon below the portrait. The surrounding design is the same as the 2-cent stamp, with the necessary change of numerals representing the denomination. The stamp is printed in black ink. The 7-cent stamp was first placed on sale at Washington, D. C., and Niles, Ohio, the birthplace of former President McKinley, on May 1, 1923.

Eight-cent.—Portrait of Grant, from photograph, with the name "Grant" on the ribbon below the portrait. The surrounding design is the same as the 2-cent stamp, with the necessary change of numerals representing the denomination. The stamp is printed in olive green ink and was placed on sale at Washington, D. C., May 1, 1923.

Nine-cent.—Portrait of Jefferson, after painting by Gilbert Stuart, with the name "Jefferson" on the ribbon below the portrait. The surrounding design is the same as the 2-cent stamp, with the necessary change of figures representing the denomination. The stamp is printed in pink ink and was placed on sale at Washington, D. C., on January 15, 1923.

Ten-cent.—Portrait of Monroe, after painting by J. Vanderlyn, with the name "Monroe" on the ribbon below the portrait. The surrounding design is the same as the 2-cent stamp, with the necessary change of numerals representing the denomination. The stamp is printed in yellow ink and was placed on sale at Washington, D. C., January 15, 1923.

Eleven-cent.—Portrait of Hayes, from photograph, with the name "Hayes" on the ribbon below the portrait. The surrounding design is the same as the 2-cent stamp, with the necessary change of numerals representing the denomination. The stamp is printed in light blue ink. The 11-cent stamp was the first denomination of the new series issued. It was first placed on sale at Washington, D. C., and Fremont, Ohio, October 4, 1922, in connection with the celebration of the one hundredth anniversary of former President Hayes' birth.

Twelve-cent.—Portrait of Cleveland, from photograph, with the name "Cleveland" on the ribbon below the portrait. The surrounding design is the same as the 2-cent stamp, with the necessary change of numerals representing the denomination. The stamp is printed in purplish brown ink. The 12-cent stamp was first placed on sale at Washington, D. C., and Caldwell, N. J., the birthplace of former President Cleveland, March 20, 1923.

Fourteen-cent.—American Indian, from photograph of "Hollow Horn Bear", a Brule Sioux chief. The words "American Indian" appear on the ribbon below the portrait. The surrounding design is the same as the 2-cent stamp except that the numeral "14" appears in the ovals in both lower corners. The stamp is printed in indigo ink. The 14-cent stamp was first placed on sale at Washington, D. C., and Muskogee, Okla., the headquarters of the Five Civilized Indian Tribes, May 1, 1923.

Fifteen-cent.—Liberty, from a photograph and drawing of Statue of Liberty with view of New York Harbor in the background. The central design is partly inclosed in a spread horseshoe panel supported at the base by acanthus scrolls. Within the panel and above the design appear the words "United States postage" in white Roman letters. On a ribbon below the design is the word "Liberty" and under this, at the bottom of the stamp, in a white-edged panel, appears the word "Cents." In both lower corners, within circles with dark backgrounds, is the white numeral "15." The entire stamp is inclosed within a single white-line border, with small panels supported by acanthus scrolls in both upper corners, and is printed in dark-gray ink and was placed on sale at Washington, D. C., on November 11, 1922.

Twenty-cent.—Golden Gate, after painting by W. A. Coulter. The design is within a semicircle surrounded by a panel which is supported on either side by acanthus scrolls. Within this panel and above the design appear the words "United States postage" in white Roman letters. On a ribbon below the design are the words "Golden Gate" and under this, at the bottom of the stamp, in a white-edged panel, appears the word "Cents." In both lower corners within circles with dark backgrounds is the white numeral "20." The entire stamp is inclosed within a single white-line border with triangular white-line ornaments in both upper corners and is printed in crimson ink. The 20-cent stamp was first placed on sale at Washington, D. C., and San Francisco, Calif., May 1, 1923.

Twenty-five-cent.—Niagara, from photograph of Niagara Falls, taken from Goat Island. The word "Niagara" appears on the ribbon below the central design. The surrounding design is the same as the 20-cent stamp except that the numeral "25" appears in the circles in both lower corners and is printed in dark-green ink and was placed on sale at Washington, D. C., November 11, 1922.

Thirty-cent.—Buffalo, from photograph. The surrounding design is the same as the 20-cent stamp except that there is no ribbon below the central design bearing the name of the subject, and the numeral "30" appears in the circles in both lower corners and is printed in sepia ink and was placed on sale at Washington, D. C., March 20, 1923.

Fifty-cent.—Arlington Amphitheatre, with Tomb of the Unknown Soldier in the foreground, from photograph and drawing, with the words "Arlington Amphitheatre" on the ribbon below the central design. The surrounding design is the same as the 20-cent stamp, with the necessary change of numerals representing the denomination. The stamp is printed in lavender ink. The 50-cent stamp was first placed on sale at the post office at Washington, D. C., November 11, 1922, Armistice Day.

One-dollar.—Lincoln Memorial, from photograph and drawing, with the words "Lincoln Memorial" on the ribbon below the central design. The surrounding design is the same as the 20-cent stamp except that the numeral "1" appears in the circles in both lower corners, and with the word "Dollar" instead of "Cents" at the bottom of the stamp. The stamp is printed in brown ink. The $1 stamp was first placed on sale at Washington, D. C., and Springfield, Ill., on Lincoln's birthday, February 12, 1923.

Two-dollar.—United States Capitol, from photograph and drawing, with the words "U. S. Capitol" on the ribbon below the central design. The surrounding design is the same as the 20-cent stamp except that the numeral "2" appears in the circles in both lower corners, with the word "Dollars" instead of "Cents" at the bottom of the stamp. The stamp is printed in blue ink and was placed on sale at Washington, D. C., on March 20, 1923.

Five-dollar.—America, from photograph of replica of Statue of Freedom surmounting the United States Capitol, with the word "America" on the ribbon below the central design. The surrounding design is the same as the 20-cent stamp except that the numeral "5" appears in the circles in both lower corners and the word "Dollars" appears at the bottom of the stamp instead of "Cents." This is the only stamp of the series printed in two colors. The central design is printed in blue ink, with the border design printed in red, and was placed on sale at Washington, D. C., on March 20, 1923.

PRECANCELED POSTAGE STAMPS—ISSUE OF 1923

Owing to the increased demand for precanceled postage stamps for use at the larger post offices, the department decided to issue such stamps which could be printed and precanceled in one operation on the rotary presses at the Bureau of Engraving and Printing, at a reduction in cost over the former method of precanceling in post offices.

The 1-cent stamp, issue of 1923, was the first denomination precanceled by the new method at the Bureau of Engraving and Printing. These stamps were for the postmaster, New York, N. Y., and were first issued April 21, 1923. The precanceling was done in black ink, as follows:

NEW YORK
N. Y.

Other postmasters were later furnished with the 1-cent stamp precanceled with the name of their post office.

It was later decided to issue *precanceled postage stamps in coils*, and on January 7, 1924, the 1-cent denomination, series of 1923, was first issued in that form to the postmaster at New York, N. Y., in coils of 500 and 1,000 stamps each, precanceled with the name of his office.

The 2-cent denomination precanceled *in coils* was first issued to the postmaster, Chicago, Ill., January 31, 1924, precanceled with the name of his office.

AIR-MAIL STAMPS—ISSUE OF 1923

Denomination	Color	Subject
8-cent	Green	Mail airplane radiator with propeller attached.
16-cent	Blue	Official insignia of the Air Mail Service.
24-cent	Red	Mail airplane in flight.

This series of air-mail stamps was issued primarily for use in the new night-flying air-mail service between New York and San Francisco.

Three zones were established in connection with this service, the first from New York to Chicago, the second from Chicago to Cheyenne, and the third from Cheyenne to San Francisco, and the rate of postage was 8 cents an ounce, or fraction thereof, for each zone, or part of zone, in which mail was carried by plane.

The stamps are about ⅞ by ¾ inch in dimension, arranged horizontally. The central design of the 8-cent stamp is a mail airplane radiator with propeller attached. Above this design in a curved panel are the words "U. S. postage" in white Roman capital letters. Triangular ornaments appear in both upper corners. Below the central design, in a straight line of Roman capital letters, is the word "Cents", with the numeral "8" within ovals in both lower corners. The 8-cent stamp is printed in green ink.

The 16-cent stamp is the same shape and size as the 8-cent stamp, and has for its central design the official insignia of the air-mail service, showing a circular design with spread wings on either side. In the center, upon a dark background, appear the letters "U. S." with the word "Air" above and the word "Mail" below. Above this central design in a curved panel are the words "U. S. postage" in white Roman capital letters. A dark shaded triangle appears in both upper corners of the stamp. Below the central design in a straight line of Roman capital letters is the word "Cents" with the numeral "16" within circles, with dark backgrounds in both lower corners. The stamp is printed in blue ink.

The 24-cent stamp is the same shape and size as the other denominations and has for its central design a mail airplane in flight. Above this design in a curved panel are the words "U. S. postage" in white Roman capital letters. Ornamental scrolls appear in both upper corners. Below the central design in a straight line of Roman capital letters is the word "Cents", with the numeral "24" within circles with dark backgrounds in both lower corners. The stamp is printed in red ink.

The new air-mail stamps were first placed on sale at the Philatelic Agency, Division of Stamps, Post Office Department, on the following dates: 8-cent, August 15, 1923; 16-cent, August 17, 1923; and 24-cent, August 21, 1923, but they were not issued to postmasters until August 24, 1923, when they were sent to 16 designated post offices, which had been selected as mailing points on the air-mail route.

Owing to the new air-mail service not having been permanently established at that time the postmasters at these offices were instructed to withhold the sale of these stamps to the public until further advised by the department. It was later decided that the new air-mail service should become effective July 1, 1924, and the air-mail stamps were accordingly placed on sale to the public *beginning June 16, 1924.*

HARDING MEMORIAL STAMP (2-CENT)—ISSUE OF 1923

As a fitting tribute to the memory of the late President Warren G. Harding, the department issued, for a limited period, a special Harding memorial stamp of the 2-cent denomination, printed in black ink.

The Harding memorial stamp is the same shape and size as the current 2-cent stamp and bears the portrait of Warren G. Harding from an etching made from a photograph, within an oval and partly inclosed in a panel, which is supported on either side by acanthus scrolls. Above the portrait within a curved panel appear the words "United States postage" in white Roman capital letters. On a ribbon below the oval is the name "Harding" and under this at the bottom of the stamp appears the word "Cents." In both lower corners within ovals with dark backgrounds is the white numeral "2." In the upper left-hand corner appears the year of birth, "1865", and in the upper right-hand corner the year of death, "1923." The entire stamp is inclosed within a plain black border.

The Harding memorial stamp was first placed on sale at Marion, Ohio, and Washington, D. C., on September 1, 1923.

The issuance of this stamp was discontinued February 27, 1924.

The Harding memorial stamp was also issued in sheets of 400 stamps each, unperforated. They were first placed on sale at the Philatelic Agency, November 15, 1923.

HUGUENOT-WALLOON TERCENTENARY STAMPS—ISSUE OF 1924

This series of postage stamps was issued to commemorate the three hundredth anniversary of the settling of Walloons in New Netherlands, now the State of New York, in 1624. The stamps were first placed on sale May 1, 1924, at Washington, D. C., and the following additional post offices: Jacksonville, Fla., Mayport, Fla., Albany, N. Y., New Rochelle, N. Y., New York, N. Y., Allentown, Pa., Lancaster, Pa., Philadelphia, Pa., Reading, Pa., and Charleston, S. C.

Denomination	Color	Subject
1-cent	Green	Ship.
2-cent	Red	Landing of the Walloons.
5-cent	Blue	Marker.

The stamps are rectangular in shape, about ⅞ by 1⅜ inches in dimension.

The 1-cent stamp has for its central design a view of the ship *New Netherland*, upon which the Walloons sailed. Above this design, in a semicircular panel, appear the words "Huguenot-Walloon Tercentenary" in white Roman letters, and above this, at the top of the stamp, in a straight line, are the words "U. S. postage." In both upper corners are ribbon scrolls bearing the years "1624" at the left and "1924" at the right. At the bottom of the stamp, in a straight line, is the word "Cent", and in both lower corners within circles with dark backgrounds is the white numeral "1." The entire stamp is inclosed within a single white-line border.

The central design of the 2-cent stamp represents the landing of the Walloons at Albany, N. Y. The surrounding design is the same as the 1-cent stamp, with the necessary change of numerals representing the denomination, and with the word "Cents" instead of "Cent."

The 5-cent stamp has for its central design the Ribault Memorial Monument located at Mayport, Fla., showing the landing place of one colony of Walloons. The surrounding design is the same as the 2-cent stamp with the necessary change of numerals representing the denomination.

This series of commemorative stamps was issued in sheets of 50.

ORDINARY POSTAGE STAMPS (½-CENT AND 1½-CENT)—ISSUE OF 1925

NEW DENOMINATIONS

The Postal Service Act approved February 28, 1925, increasing the rates of postage effective April 15, 1925, made it necessary to issue a new ½-cent and a 1½-cent ordinary postage stamp.

These new stamps are the same shape and size as the 1-cent ordinary stamp of the current series, issue of 1922–23. The ½-cent stamp bears the portrait of Nathan Hale, with the name "Nathan Hale" on a ribbon below the portrait. The surrounding design is the same as the 1-cent stamp except that the numeral "½" appears in the ovals in both lower corners. The stamp is inclosed within a cross-line border and is printed in sepia.

The ½-cent stamp was first placed on sale April 4, 1925, at New Haven, Conn., and Washington, D. C.

The 1½-cent stamp bears the portrait of the late President Warren G. Harding with the name "Harding" on a ribbon below the portrait. The surrounding design is the same as the current 2-cent stamp, except that the numeral "1½" appears in the ovals in both lower corners and the triangular ornaments in both upper corners were changed. The stamp is inclosed within a plain border and is printed in light brown.

The 1½-cent stamp was first placed on sale March 19, 1925, at Washington, D. C.

LEXINGTON-CONCORD COMMEMORATIVE STAMPS—ISSUE OF 1925

This series of postage stamps was issued to commemorate the one hundred and fiftieth anniversary of the Battle of Lexington and Concord. They were first placed on sale April 4, 1925, at Washington, D. C., and the following additional post offices: Concord, Mass., Concord Junction, Mass., Boston, Mass., Cambridge, Mass., Lexington, Mass.

Denomination	Color	Subject
1-cent	Green	Washington at Cambridge.
2-cent	Red	Birth of Liberty.
5-cent	Blue	The Minute Man.

The stamps are rectangular in shape, about $\frac{13}{16}$ by $1\frac{7}{16}$ inches in dimension.

The subject of the 1-cent stamp is "Washington at Cambridge" from a photoglyphic chart in the possession of the Cambridge Public Library and represents Washington taking command of the American Army. The title appears in small white letters under the central design. Beneath this, on a ribbon scroll, appear the words "Lexington-Concord", and at the bottom of the stamp are the words "One cent." In a straight line, at the top of the stamp, appear the words "United States postage" in white Roman letters, and in both lower corners, within circles, is the white numeral "1." Above the circles are the years "1775" at the left and "1925" at the right, and in panels arranged at the right and left of the central design are two muskets with powder-horns. The entire design is inclosed within a straight line border and is printed in green ink.

The subject of the 2-cent stamp is "Birth of Liberty" from the painting by Henry Sandham in the town hall at Lexington and represents the Battle of Lexington and Concord. The title appears in small white letters under the central design. The surrounding design is the same as the 1-cent stamp except that the numeral "2" appears in the circles and the words "Two cents" appear at the bottom of the stamp. This stamp is printed in red ink.

The subject of the 5-cent stamp is "The Minute Man" from a photograph of the statue located at Concord, Mass. The title appears in small dark letters under the central design, which stands between two columns. To the right and left of the columns are two tablets bearing the following inscription: "By the rude bridge that arched the flood their flag to April's breeze unfurled. Here once the embattled farmers stood and fired the shot heard round the world." The surrounding design is the same as the other denominations except that the numeral "5" appears in the circles and the words "Five cents" appear at the bottom of the stamp. This stamp is printed in blue ink.

This series of commemorative stamps was issued in sheets of 50.

SPECIAL-DELIVERY STAMPS (15-CENT AND 20-CENT)—ISSUE OF 1925

NEW DENOMINATIONS

Two new special-delivery stamps for use on parcels subject to the increased special-delivery fees, as provided under the act of February 28, 1925, were issued by the department. These stamps are of the 15-cent and 20-cent denominations, and are described as follows:

The 15-cent special-delivery stamp is printed in orange and is the same shape, size, and design as the current 10-cent special-delivery stamp, except that the numerals "15" appear in both lower corners and the words "Fifteen cents" appear in the panel at the bottom of the stamp.

This stamp was first placed on sale April 11, 1925, at Washington, D. C.

The 20-cent special-delivery stamp is the same shape and size as the current 10-cent special-delivery stamp. The central design is a motor truck standing at the post office with a carrier loading parcel-post packages for special delivery. At the top of the stamp, upon a curved ribbon, are the words "Special delivery" in dark letters with the words "U. S. postage" directly beneath the ribbon in white letters. Above the motor truck are the words "At any United States post office", and at the bottom of the stamp, within a panel, are the words "Twenty cents." In both upper corners, upon ribbon scrolls, are the numerals "20" and in both lower corners, within circles, are the white numerals "20." The stamp is inclosed within a cross-line border and is printed in black ink.

The 20-cent special-delivery stamp was first placed on sale April 25, 1925, at Washington, D. C.

SPECIAL-HANDLING STAMP (25-CENT)—ISSUE OF 1925

The Postal Service act, approved February 28, 1925, provided for a special-handling stamp of 25-cent denomination for use on fourth-class mail matter, which would secure for such mail matter the expeditious handling accorded to mail matter of the first class. A description follows:

The 25-cent special-handling stamp is the same shape and size as the special-delivery stamp, but of entirely different design. Within a circle in the center of the stamp is the numeral "25" with the words "Special handling" arranged in a semicircle directly above. At the top of the stamp, in a straight line, are the words "United States postage" and at the bottom, within a panel, is the word "Cents." The background is of ornamental lathe work and the entire stamp is inclosed within a straight-line border. This stamp is printed in dark green and was first placed on sale April 11, 1925, at Washington, D. C.

POSTAGE-DUE STAMP (½-CENT)—ISSUE OF 1925

NEW DENOMINATION

On April 13, 1925, the department issued a new ½-cent postage-due stamp to be used in the collection of postage on short-paid third-class matter.

The new stamp is the same shape, size, and design as the current series of postage-due stamps, issue of 1894, except that the white numeral "½" appears in the center of the stamp and the words "Half cent" appear in the panel at the bottom. The color is claret.

NORSE-AMERICAN COMMEMORATIVE STAMPS (2-CENT AND 5-CENT)—ISSUE OF 1925

These stamps were issued to commemorate the one-hundredth anniversary of the arrival in New York, on October 9, 1825, of the sloop *Restaurationen* with the first group of immigrants to the United States from Norway.

The stamps are in two denominations, 2-cent and 5-cent, and are described as follows:

They are the same size, $^{75}/_{100}$ by $^{87}/_{100}$ inch, as the ordinary series of postage stamps, but with horizontal design, printed in two colors.

The 2-cent stamp has for its central design a ship representing the sloop *Restaurationen*, with a smaller vessel in the background, from a photoengraving. At the top of the stamp, in a straight panel, appear the words "Norse-American" in white Roman letters, and below this, on a curved ribbon, is the word "Centennial" in dark letters. Ribbon scrolls appear in the upper portion on each side of the stamp with the years "1825" at the left and "1925" at the right. At the bottom of the stamp, in three straight lines, are the words "United States postage, two cents", and in both lower corners, within circles with dark backgrounds, is the white numeral "2." The central design is printed in black with the border design printed in red.

The 5-cent stamp has for its central design a Viking ship from a photoengraving. At the top of the stamp, in white Gothic letters, appear the words "Norse-American" and below this, on a curved ribbon, is the word "Centennial" in dark letters. At the left of the stamp is a shield of Norway with the year "1825" above, and at the right of the stamp is a shield of the United States with the year "1925" above. Below the central design, in three straight lines, are the words "United States postage, five cents", and in both lower corners, within circles with dark backgrounds, is the white numeral "5." The central design is printed in black with the border design printed in blue.

The first issue of the Norse-American commemorative stamps was placed on sale May 18, 1925, at the following post offices: St. Paul, Minneapolis, Benson, and Northfield, Minn.; Algona and Decorah, Iowa; and Washington, D. C.

ORDINARY POSTAGE STAMP (17-CENT)—ISSUE OF 1925

NEW DENOMINATION

A new postage stamp of 17-cent denomination, bearing the portrait of Woodrow Wilson, was issued and first placed on sale December 28, 1925, at Washington, D. C., Princeton, N. J., New York, N. Y., and Staunton, Va.

The stamp is the same shape and size, a horizontal rectangle, as the 20-cent stamp of the current series and is printed in bank note black ink. The central design is a portrait of Woodrow Wilson within a semicircle and is partly inclosed in a panel which is supported on either side by acanthus scrolls. Within this panel and above the portrait appear the words "United States postage" in white Roman letters. On a ribbon below the portrait is the name "Wilson" and under this, at the bottom of the stamp, appears the word "Cents." In both lower corners, within circles with dark backgrounds, are the white numerals "17." Triangular white-line ornaments appear in both upper corners and the entire stamp is inclosed within a single white-line border.

The new stamp was issued primarily for use in prepaying a single rate of letter postage and registry fee and was also available to the amount of its value for other purposes for which ordinary postage stamps are used.

ORDINARY POSTAGE STAMP (13-CENT)—ISSUE OF 1926

A new postage stamp of 13-cent denomination was issued and first placed on sale January 11, 1926, at Washington, D. C., and Indianapolis, Ind.

The stamp is the same shape and size, $75/100$ by $87/100$ inch, as the 12-cent stamp of the current series and is printed in green ink. The central design is a portrait of Benjamin Harrison within an oval with open background and is partly inclosed in a panel which is supported on either side by acanthus scrolls. Above the portrait, in a curved line, appear the words "United States postage" in white Roman letters. On a ribbon below the oval is the name "Harrison", and under this, at the bottom of the stamp, appears the word "Cents." In both lower corners, within ovals with dark backgrounds, are the white numerals "13." The entire stamp is inclosed within a cross-line border with small triangular ornaments in both upper corners.

This stamp was issued primarily for use in prepaying postage on parcels and postage and insurance fee on insured parcels amounting to 13 cents.

AIR-MAIL STAMP (10-CENT)—ISSUE OF 1926

NEW DENOMINATION

The act of Congress approved February 2, 1925, making the rate of postage on air mail, carried on contract air-mail routes, not less than 10 cents for each ounce or fraction thereof, made it necessary to issue a new 10-cent air-mail stamp.

This stamp is a horizontal rectangle $75/100$ by $184/100$ inches in size and is printed in blue ink. The central design represents a relief map of the United States, showing some of the rivers and mountain ranges. On each side is an airplane in flight, one traveling east and the other toward the west. Across the top of the stamp, in white Roman letters, are the words "United States postage", with the words "Air mail" directly beneath. At the bottom of the stamp, in shaded letters, is the word "Cents", and in both lower corners are the white numerals "10." Ornamental plastic brackets appear at each side of the stamp.

The new air mail stamp was first placed on sale February 13, 1926, at the post offices at Detroit and Dearborn, Mich., Chicago, Ill., Cleveland, Ohio, and Washington, D. C.

SESQUICENTENNIAL COMMEMORATIVE STAMP (2-CENT)—ISSUE OF 1926

A new postage stamp of 2-cent denomination was issued to commemorate the one hundred and fiftieth anniversary of American independence and in connection with the Sesquicentennial Exposition held in Philadelphia in 1926.

The stamp is a horizontal rectangle of the same size as the special-delivery stamp, $84/100$ by $144/100$ inches, and is printed in red ink. The central design is the Liberty Bell, which swings from the tops of four flat ornamental columns that rest on the lower panel. The words "Sesquicentennial Exposition" appear across the top of the stamp in a straight line, with a ruled shadow background. Under these in a curved panel appear the words "United States postage." This panel is supported at either end by a scroll extending out of circular panels at either lower corner. Within these circular panels appears the numeral "2." Across the bottom of the stamp are the words "Two cents" within a horizontal panel. In the upper corners under the words "Sesquicentennial Exposition" appear the dates "1776" at the left and "1926" at the right. All the lettering on the stamp is white-faced Roman.

The sesquicentennial stamp was first placed on sale May 10, 1926, at the post offices at Philadelphia, Pa., Boston, Mass., and Washington, D. C.

ERICSSON MEMORIAL STAMP (5-CENT)—ISSUE OF 1926

A new postage stamp of 5-cent denomination was issued as a memorial to John Ericsson, builder of the *Monitor,* and in connection with the unveiling of his statue by the Crown Prince of Sweden at Washington, D. C., on May 29, 1926.

The subject of this stamp is a model similar to the John Ericsson memorial statue designed by J. E. Fraser.

The new stamp is an upright rectangle, $1^{44}/_{100}$ by $^{84}/_{100}$ inches in size, printed in purplish blue ink. The central design is the white marble figure of 'John Ericsson seated in a large chair resting on a stone base. Upon the base appear the words "John Ericsson Memorial" and "Cents" in white Gothic letters with the numeral "5" in both corners. Extending from either side and in rear of chair on darker stone appear the years of his birth and death, "1803–1889." On an ornate base, above and to the rear of the figure of Ericsson, is a group of allegorical figures in white marble, of which only the center one, representing "Vision", is shown. The background for this statue is a dark sky with darkly silhouetted evergreens showing on each side. A narrow white line border surrounds the stamp with a shield of the United States in the upper left corner and a shield of Sweden in the upper right corner. Connecting the two shields is a panel supported on each side by small ornamental brackets and containing the words "U. S. postage" in white-face Gothic letters.

The Ericsson stamp was first placed on sale May 29, 1926, at the post offices at New York, N. Y., Chicago, Ill., Minneapolis, Minn., and Washington, D. C.

AIR-MAIL STAMP (15-CENT)—ISSUE OF 1926

NEW DENOMINATION

A new air-mail stamp of 15-cent denomination was issued for use in the contract air-mail service and first placed on sale at Washington, D. C., September 18, 1926. This stamp is the same shape, size, and design as the current 10-cent air-mail stamp, issued in February, in accordance with act of Congress approved February 2, 1925, except that the numerals "15" appear in both lower corners of the stamp and it is printed in sepia.

BATTLE OF WHITE PLAINS COMMEMORATIVE STAMP (2-CENT)—
ISSUE OF 1926

This stamp of 2-cent denomination was issued to commemorate the one hundred and fiftieth anniversary of the Battle of White Plains.

The new stamp is a horizontal rectangle, $75/100$ by $87/100$ inch in size, and is printed in red ink. The center vignette shows a gun crew in action, consisting of four men dressed in Continental uniform, with cannon and ammunition, copied from a painting by E. F. Ward, submitted by Dr. Jason S. Parker, of White Plains, N. Y. Over the vignette, in ribbon form, are the words "United States postage" in Roman letters. In the upper left corner appears the year "1776" and in the upper right corner the year "1926." Below the vignette in the center of the stamp is a circle containing the large numeral "2", with the word "Cents" on both sides, and above the circle are the words "Battle of White Plains." In the lower left corner is the Continental flag and in the lower right corner the historic "Liberty or Death" flag, first used in the Battle of White Plains, both appearing in oblique position.

This stamp was first placed on sale October 18, 1926, at the post office at White Plains, N. Y., and for the benefit of philatelists it was also placed on sale the same date at the branch of the department's Philatelic Agency which was temporarily established at the International Philatelic Exhibition held at Grand Central Palace, New York City, from October 16 to 23, inclusive. On October 28, 1926, the anniversary of the Battle of White Plains, the new stamp was placed on sale at the Philatelic Agency at Washington, D. C., and at a number of the larger post offices.

The Battle of White Plains stamp was also issued in special sheets of 25 stamps each, with the inscription "International Philatelic Exhibition, October 16 to 23, 1926, New York, N. Y., U. S. A.", appearing on the margins of each sheet. These sheets were all printed, gummed, and perforated at the Bureau of Engraving and Printing, and sent to the branch Philatelic Agency at the International Philatelic Exhibition, to be placed on sale October 18, 1926, the same date the regular sheets containing 100 stamps were placed on sale. These special sheets were also placed on sale at the Philatelic Agency at Washington, D. C., on October 28, 1926. They were not issued to postmasters for sale to the public.

As a special feature of the International Philatelic Exhibition, the Bureau of Engraving and Printing installed a hand-roller press and printed 700 sheets of White Plains stamps from plate No. 18772. These sheets, containing four blocks of 25 stamps each, were not gummed or perforated, and none was sold. They were all returned to the Bureau of Engraving and Printing and destroyed by a special committee appointed for that purpose. At the same time plate No. 18772, from which they were printed, was mutilated and later destroyed.

AIR-MAIL STAMP (20-CENT)—ISSUE OF 1927

NEW DENOMINATION

Owing to the new rate of postage on air mail, effective February 1, 1927, the department issued a new 20-cent air-mail stamp, which was first placed on sale at New York, N. Y., and Washington, D. C., January 25, 1927. This stamp is the same shape, size, and design as the current 10-cent and 15-cent air-mail stamps, except that the numerals "20" appear in both lower corners of the stamp and it is printed in green.

LINDBERGH AIR-MAIL STAMP (10-CENT)—ISSUE OF 1927

As a special tribute to Col. Charles A. Lindbergh, the intrepid air-mail pilot who made the first nonstop flight from New York to Paris, the department issued a new 10-cent air-mail stamp which temporarily displaced the current 10-cent air-mail stamp, issue of 1926.

The new stamp is the same shape and size, $75/100$ by $184/100$ inches, as the current air-mail stamps, and is printed in blue. The central design represents Lindbergh's airplane, *The Spirit of Saint Louis*, in flight. Across the top of the stamp, in white Roman letters, are the words "United States postage", with the words "Lindbergh air mail" directly beneath. At the left of the central design appears the coast line of the North American Continent, with the words "New York" in small dark letters, and to the right appears the coast line of Europe, showing Ireland, Great Britain, and France, with the word "Paris", also in small dark letters. A dotted line depicting the course of the flight to France connects the two cities. At the bottom of the stamp, in shaded letters, is the words "Cents", and in both lower corners are the white numerals "10." The stamp is inclosed within a straight-line border.

The 10-cent Lindbergh air-mail stamp was first placed on sale June 18, 1927, at the post offices at St. Louis, Mo., Detroit, Mich., Little Falls, Minn., and Washington, D. C. This stamp was also issued in books of 6 stamps, which were first placed on sale at Washington, D. C., and Cleveland, Ohio, on May 26, 1928.

BURGOYNE CAMPAIGN COMMEMORATIVE STAMP (2-CENT)—ISSUE OF 1927

This new postage stamp of 2-cent denomination was issued to commemorate the Battles of Fort Stanwix, Oriskany, Bennington, and Saratoga.

The stamp is the same shape and size as the special-delivery stamp, $84/100$ by $1 44/100$ inches and is printed in red ink. The central design represents the surrender of General Burgoyne, and is inclosed in panels bearing the words "Fort Stanwix" at the left, "Oriskany" at the top, and "Bennington" at the right, with the word "Saratoga" beneath the design. In a curved panel near the top of the stamp are the words "U. S. postage" in white Roman letters, and on ribbon scrolls in both upper corners are the years "1777" and "1927." In an ornamental panel at the bottom of the stamp appears the word "Cents" with the numeral "2" in both lower corners within circles supported by acanthus scrolls. Immediately beneath the central vignette appear the words "Surrender of Genl. Burgoyne."

The Burgoyne campaign stamp was first placed on sale August 3, 1927, at Albany, Rome, Syracuse, and Utica, N. Y., and Washington, D. C.

VERMONT SESQUICENTENNIAL STAMP (2-CENT)—ISSUE OF 1927

This postage stamp of 2-cent denomination was issued to commemorate the one hundred and fiftieth anniversary of the independence of Vermont and the Battle of Bennington.

This stamp is the same shape and size as the ordinary stamp, $75/100$ by $87/100$ inch, and is printed in red ink. The central design represents a Green Mountain Boy dressed in buckskin leaning on his rifle. Across the top of the stamp in a straight line are the words "Vermont Sesquicentennial" in small block letters, and in an arched panel supported by small ornamental brackets are the words "U. S. postage" in white Roman letters. On ribbon scrolls in both upper corners appear the years "1777" at the left and "1927" at the right. Within circles in both lower corners is the white numeral "2" with the word "Cents" in a panel connecting the circles. To the left of the central design is a loose ribbon bearing the word "Bennington" in small Roman letters.

The Vermont Sesquicentennial stamp was first placed on sale August 3, 1927, at Bennington, Vt., and Washington, D. C.

VALLEY FORGE COMMEMORATIVE STAMP (2-CENT)—ISSUE OF 1928

The Valley Forge stamp was issued to commemorate the one hundred and fiftieth anniversary of the encampment of Washington's Army at Valley Forge during the winter of 1777–78.

The new stamp is the same shape and size as the ordinary stamp, $75/100$ by $87/100$ inch, and is printed in red ink. The vignette shows Washington kneeling in prayer. Across the top of the stamp in a straight line are the words "U. S. postage" in white Roman letters, and on a ribbon above the vignette are the words "Valley Forge" with the years "1778" and "1928." The white numeral "2" appears in both lower corners within circles, which are connected by a panel bearing the word "Cents." On a ribbon above the panel are the words "In God We Trust" in small Gothic letters.

The Valley Forge commemorative stamp was first placed on sale May 26, 1928, at Cleveland, Ohio, Valley Forge, Philadelphia, Lancaster, Norristown, and West Chester, Pa., and Washington, D. C.

HAWAIIAN SURCHARGED STAMPS (2-CENT AND 5-CENT)—ISSUE OF 1928

A special issue of surcharged postage stamps was provided for placing on sale in Hawaiian post offices in connection with the sesquicentennial celebration held August 15 to 20, 1928.

The issue was prepared by overprinting a quantity of 2-cent and 5-cent stamps of the 1922–23 series, with the surcharge "Hawaii" across the upper half of the stamp, and the dates "1778–1928" below. The surcharge was in black ink on both stamps.

The surcharged stamps were first placed on sale August 13, 1928, in Honolulu, Hawaii, and at other Hawaiian post offices as soon thereafter as distribution could be made.

The surcharged stamps were not issued to post offices outside of the Hawaiian Islands, but a limited supply was placed on sale in the Philatelic Agency for the convenience of stamp collectors.

The Hawaiian surcharged stamps are valid for the prepayment of postage at all post offices using ordinary United States stamps.

SPECIAL HANDLING STAMPS—ISSUE OF 1928

Special-handling stamps in denominations of 10, 15, and 20 cents were required to conform to the rates provided by postal legislation, effective July 1, 1928.

The new special-handling stamps are of the same size and shape as the discontinued 25-cent special-handling stamp and have within a circle in the center of each stamp the numbers "10", "15", or "20", with the words "Special handling" arranged in a semicircle directly above. At the top of the stamp in a straight line are the words "United States postage" and at the bottom, within a panel, is the word "Cents." The background is of ornamental lathe work and the entire stamp is inclosed within a straight-line border. The color is dark green.

The new special-handling stamps were first placed on sale at Washington, D. C., on June 25, 1928.

AIR-MAIL STAMP (5-CENT)—ISSUE OF 1928

The 5-cent air-mail stamp was issued to meet the new rate of postage on air-mail matter, effective August 1, 1928.

The stamp is a horizontal rectangle $1\frac{8}{32}$ by $1\frac{15}{32}$ inches in size and is printed in two colors, the outer border in red and the vignette in blue. The central design represents the beacon light on Sherman Hill, in the Rocky Mountains, with a mail plane in flight at the left. In a panel at the top of the stamp are the words "U. S. postage" in white Roman letters, and on ribbons directly beneath, supported by acanthus scrolls, are the words "Air" on the left and "Mail" on the right. Ornamental designs appear in both upper corners, and in both lower corners, within circles with dark backgrounds, is the white numeral "5." A white bordered panel at the bottom of the stamp contains the word "Cents" in white Roman letters.

The 5-cent air-mail stamp was first placed on sale July 25, 1928, at Washington, D. C.

MONMOUTH COMMEMORATIVE STAMP (2-CENT)—ISSUE OF 1928

This stamp was issued to commemorate the one hundred and fiftieth anniversary of the Battle of Monmouth and as a memorial to Molly Pitcher, the popular heroine of the engagement.

The issue consists of ordinary 2-cent stamps of the current series overprinted with the words "Molly Pitcher" arranged in two horizontal lines across the face of the stamp. The surcharge is in black.

The surcharged Monmouth anniversary stamps were first offered for sale October 20, 1928, at the post offices in Freehold, N. J., Red Bank, N. J., and Washington, D. C.

INTERNATIONAL CIVIL AERONAUTICS CONFERENCE COMMEMORATIVE STAMPS (2-CENT AND 5-CENT)—ISSUE OF 1928

This series of special stamps was issued in connection with the International Civil Aeronautics Conference, which was held in Washington, D. C., on December 12, 13, and 14, 1928, on the call of President Coolidge.

The stamps are the same shape and size as the special-delivery stamp, $\frac{84}{100}$ by $1\frac{44}{100}$ inches. The 2-cent stamp is printed in red and the 5-cent stamp in blue. The stamps are inclosed at the top and sides in a dark border panel with the wording "U. S. postage" in white Roman lettering along the upper edge with a small scroll at each end.　Under the panel in small solid architectural Roman lettering are the words "International Civil Aeronautics Conference."　On either side of the central designs are shown on the left the Washington Monument, and on the right the United States Capitol.　In both lower corners are rectangular shields containing the denomination numerals "2" or "5" in white.　In a ribbon panel with folded ends between the numerals are the dates "December 12, 13, 14, 1928."　Under the ribbon is a base panel with the word "Cents" in white Roman lettering.

The central design of the 2-cent stamp shows the airplane used by the Wright brothers in their first successful flight at Kitty Hawk, N. C.　The 5-cent stamp has for the central design a modern monoplane in flight with an outline of the globe in the background.

The stamps were first placed on sale December 12, 1928, in Washington, D. C.

GEORGE ROGERS CLARK COMMEMORATIVE STAMP (2-CENT)—ISSUE OF 1929

The George Rogers Clark stamp was issued to commemorate the one hundred and fiftieth anniversary of the surrender of Fort Sackville near the present site of the city of Vincennes, Ind.

The stamp is the same shape and size as the 5-cent air-mail stamp, $1\frac{3}{32}$ by $1\frac{15}{32}$ inches, and is printed in two colors; the border in red and the vignette in black.　The central design shows the surrender of Fort Sackville to George Rogers Clark, reproduced from a photograph of the painting by Frederick C. Yohn.　The word "Vincennes" appears beneath the central design and at the top of the stamp are the words "U. S. postage" in white Roman letters.　Above the vignette is a ribbon bearing the words "George Rogers Clark" with the word "Commemorative" in a curved panel directly beneath.　In panels on either side of the stamp are acanthus scrolls and in the upper corners are the dates "1779" at the left and "1929" at the right.　In both lower corners within circles with dark backgrounds is the white numeral "2" with the word "Cents" at the bottom of the stamp.

The first day sale of the stamp on February 25, 1929, was restricted to the post office in Vincennes, Ind.

STATE SURCHARGED STAMPS—ISSUE OF 1929

This special issue of postage stamps was prepared by overprinting the abbreviations "Kans." and "Nebr." on stamps of the 1922–23 series in denominations of 1 to 10 cents, inclusive, for placing on sale in all post offices in the respective States with the exception of Kansas City, Topeka, and Wichita, Kans., Lincoln and Omaha, Nebr.　The surcharge was printed in black ink across the lower half of the stamps.　The State surcharged stamps were first placed on sale May 1, 1929, in the Philatelic Agency.

This special issue of surcharged stamps was authorized as a measure of preventing losses from post-office burglaries.　Approximately a year's supply of the stamps was printed and issued to postmasters in the respective States.　The department found it desirable to discontinue the State surcharged stamps after the initial supply was used.

EDISON COMMEMORATIVE STAMP (2-CENT)—ISSUE OF 1929

This stamp was issued to commemorate the fiftieth anniversary of the invention of the first incandescent electric lamp by Thomas Alva Edison.

The stamp is the same size as the 2-cent ordinary stamp, $^{75}/_{100}$ by $^{87}/_{100}$ inch, and is printed in red ink. The central design is a picture of the original lamp with rays issuing therefrom. Immediately above and partly encircling the lamp is a ribbon with the words "Edison's First Lamp"; above this and reaching the top of the stamp is a semicircular panel with the words "United States postage" in white Roman letters. In both upper corners are ribbon scrolls with the year "1879" at the left and "1929" at the right. On either side of the lamp and through the rays of light appears the following legend: "Electric Light's Golden Jubilee." The white numeral "2" appears in both lower corners within dark circles, which are connected by a dark panel forming the base of the stamp and containing the word "Cents" in white Roman letters.

The Edison commemorative stamp was first placed on sale June 5, 1929, at the post office at Menlo Park, N. J. The stamp was issued in both flat plate and rotary sheets containing 100 stamps each; also in sidewise coils of 500 and 3,000 stamps.

SULLIVAN EXPEDITION COMMEMORATIVE STAMP (2-CENT)—ISSUE OF 1929

This special stamp was issued to commemorate the one hundred and fiftieth anniversary of the Sullivan expedition in New York State during the Revolutionary War. The stamp is the same size as the regular issue, $^{75}/_{100}$ by $^{87}/_{100}$ inch, and is printed in red ink.

The central design is a half-length portrait of Major General Sullivan in Continental uniform over which in a semicircular panel appear the words "United States postage" in white Roman letters, on a dark background with white edges. This panel is supported on either side by brackets of scroll work forming the upper part of a narrow panel and ending at the base in dark circles with white borders. Within the circles in each lower corner appears the white numeral "2." Across the top of the stamp is a ribbon bearing the title "Sullivan Expedition" in dark architectural Roman letters. Below, in similar lettering, on either side on extensions of the ribbon panel are the dates "1779" at the left and "1929" at the right. A dark panel with white edges bearing the word "Cents" in white Roman letters connects the circles inclosing the denomination numerals. Above this base in a ribbon panel appears the wording "Maj. Gen. Sullivan" in dark Gothic letters. The entire stamp is inclosed in a narrow white border.

The Sullivan expedition commemorative stamp was first placed on sale June 17, 1929, at the following post offices: Auburn, Binghamton, Canandaigua, Canajoharie, Elmira, Geneseo, Geneva, Horseheads, Owego, Penn Yan, Perry, Seneca Falls, Waterloo, Watkins Glen, and Waverly, N. Y.

BATTLE OF FALLEN TIMBERS COMMEMORATIVE STAMP (2-CENT)— ISSUE OF 1929

This stamp was issued as a memorial to Gen. Anthony Wayne and to commemorate the one hundred and thirty-fifth anniversary of the Battle of Fallen Timbers, which culminated his military campaign against hostile Indian tribes in the Northwest Territory. The stamp is of the same size as the regular issue, $^{75}/_{100}$ by $^{87}/_{100}$ inch, and is printed in red ink.

The central design of the stamp is a reproduction in white on a dark background of the memorial group on the monument erected on the site of the battlefield, containing the figure of General Wayne in the center with an Indian on the left and a frontiersman on the right. A tablet below contains the legend, "Gen. Anthony Wayne Memorial." On the extreme upper edge of the stamp in a dark panel with white Roman lettering appear the words "United States postage." Below in a semicircular panel with white edges and white Roman lettering on a dark background are the words "Battle of Fallen Timbers." The ends of this panel are supported by uprights in the form of acanthus scrolls which end at the two lower corners in ovals having white edges and dark background. Within these ovals is the numeral "2." The ovals are connected by a base panel in dark color with the word "Cents" in white Roman letters. Between the upper horizontal and semicircular panels are white ribbons with the dates "1794" at the left and "1929" at the right in dark lettering.

The Battle of Fallen Timbers stamp was first placed on sale September 14, 1929, the date of the unveiling of the monument, at the post offices in Maumee, Perrysburg, Toledo, and Waterville, Ohio, and Erie, Pa.

OHIO RIVER CANALIZATION COMMEMORATIVE STAMP (2-CENT)— ISSUE OF 1929

This stamp commemorates the completion of the Ohio River canalization project between Cairo, Ill., and Pittsburgh, Pa.

The stamp is the same size as the regular issue, $^{75}/_{100}$ by $^{87}/_{100}$ inch, but with horizontal design, and is printed in red ink. The central design represents an Ohio River lock with surrounding scenery. At the top of the stamp within a dark panel in white Roman letters appear the words "United States postage." Below on a ribbon scroll are the words "Ohio River Canalization." In both upper corners on extensions of the ribbon scroll are the dates "1875" at the left and "1929" at the right. At the bottom of the stamp in a dark panel with white edges is the word "Cents" in white Roman letters, and in both lower corners within circles with dark backgrounds appears the white numeral "2." The entire stamp is inclosed in a narrow white border.

The Ohio River canalization stamp was first placed on sale October 19, 1929, at the post offices at Cairo, Ill., Evansville, Ind., Louisville, Ky., Cincinnati, Ohio, Homestead, Pa., Pittsburgh, Pa., and Wheeling, W. Va.

AIR-MAIL STAMP (5-CENT)—ISSUE OF 1930

This new 5-cent air-mail stamp displaced the current bicolored air-mail stamp, known as the issue of 1928.

The new stamp is the same shape and size, $^{75}/_{100}$ by $1^{84}/_{100}$ inches, as the current 10-, 15-, and 20-cent air-mail stamps and is printed in purple. The central design is a reproduction of the insignia of an air-mail pilot, a globe with extended wings on either side, with a background of rays of light. Upon the globe are the words "U. S. air mail." In a horizontal panel across the top of the stamp are the words "United States postage" in white Roman letters and at the bottom in an ornate panel is the word "Cents." The white numeral "5" appears within circles in both lower corners.

This new air-mail stamp was first placed on sale February 10, 1930, at Washington, D. C.

MASSACHUSETTS BAY COLONY COMMEMORATIVE STAMP (2-CENT)— ISSUE OF 1930

This special stamp commemorates the three hundredth anniversary of the founding of the Massachusetts Bay Colony.

The stamp is an upright rectangle the same size as the current 2-cent stamp and is printed in red ink. In a straight line across the top of the stamp are the words "United States postage" in white Roman letters, and directly beneath is a semicircular panel containing the words "Massachusetts Bay Colony." This panel is supported on either side by small acanthus-leaf brackets. In both lower corners within ovals with dark background appears the white numeral "2" and these ovals are connected by a panel bearing the word "Cents" in white Roman letters. The central design is the colonial seal with the figure of an Indian holding a bow in his left hand and an arrow in his right. On either side of the figure is a small pine tree. The years "1630" and "1930" in dark numerals are shown outside the lower part of the seal following the curve of the oval.

The Massachusetts Bay Colony stamp was first placed on sale April 8, 1930, at Boston and Salem, Mass.

CHARLESTON (S. C.) COMMEMORATIVE STAMP (2-CENT)—ISSUE OF 1930

This stamp was issued to commemorate the two hundred and sixtieth anniversary of the founding of the Province of Carolina, as well as the two hundred and fiftieth anniversary of the establishment of the original settlement near the site of the present city of Charleston, S. C.

This stamp is the same size as the current 2-cent ordinary postage stamp and is printed in red ink. In the upper half of the stamp is a semicircular ribbon bearing the words "United States postage" in dark Roman letters, while in a similar ribbon in the lower half are the words "Charleston, S. C." In the space between the central oval and the sides of the stamp are specimens of rice and indigo plants, with the names thereof indicated in dark Gothic letters on white ribbon panels. In the upper corners are the years "1680" at the left and "1930" at the right, in white numerals, and in both lower corners in small ovals appears the white numeral "2." Connecting these ovals is a panel containing the word "Cents" in white Roman letters. The central design depicts the figures of a colonial governor and a friendly Indian standing on the beach, with two ships anchored in the bay. Under the figures in a straight line is the wording "250th anniversary."

The Charleston stamp was first placed on sale April 10, 1930, at Charleston, S. C.

"GRAF ZEPPELIN" AIR-MAIL STAMPS—ISSUE OF 1930

This special series of air-mail stamps was issued for use on mail matter carried on the first Europe-Pan American round-trip flight of the Graf Zeppelin in May 1930. This series contains three stamps in denominations of 65 cents, $1.30, and $2.60.

The stamps are the same shape and size as the current air-mail stamps, $^{75}/_{100}$ by $1^{84}/_{100}$ inches, and are described as follows:

The border design is the same for each stamp, with the necessary change of numerals representing the value. At the top of the stamp in a straight line are the words "Graf Zeppelin" with the words "Europe-Pan America flight" directly beneath. At the bottom of the stamp in a dark panel appear the words "United States postage" and within circles in both lower corners are the numerals showing the denomination.

The 65-cent stamp is printed in green and contains as the central design a representation of the *Graf Zeppelin* in flight across the Atlantic Ocean in an eastward direction.

In the $1.30 stamp the airship is shown sailing westward between partial outlines of the eastern and western continents. This stamp is printed in brown.

The design of the $2.60 stamp shows the *Graf Zeppelin* emerging from the clouds, passing a globe representing the earth, and traveling toward the West. This stamp is printed in blue.

The *Graf Zeppelin* stamps were first placed on sale at the post office, Washington, D. C., and the Philatelic Agency on April 19, 1930. The stamps were placed on sale at the following additional post offices on April 21, 1930:

Alabama—Birmingham.
Arizona—Phoenix.
Arkansas—Little Rock.
California—Los Angeles, Oakland, and San Francisco.
Colorado—Denver.
Connecticut—Bridgeport, Hartford, and New Haven.
Delaware—Wilmington.
Florida—Jacksonville, Miami, and Tampa.
Georgia—Atlanta and Savannah.
Idaho—Boise.
Illinois—Chicago, Peoria, and Springfield.
Indiana—Fort Wayne, Indianapolis, and South Bend.
Iowa—Cedar Rapids, Des Moines, and Sioux City.
Kansas—Topeka and Wichita.
Kentucky—Louisville.
Louisiana—New Orleans.
Maine—Portland.
Maryland—Baltimore.
Massachusetts—Boston, Springfield, and Worcester.
Michigan—Detroit, Grand Rapids, and Lansing.
Minnesota—Duluth, Minneapolis, and St. Paul.
Mississippi—Vicksburg.
Missouri—Kansas City, St. Joseph, and St. Louis.
Montana—Helena.

Nebraska—Lincoln and Omaha.
Nevada—Reno.
New Hampshire—Concord.
New Jersey—Jersey City, Newark, and Trenton.
New Mexico—Albuquerque.
New York—Albany, Brooklyn, Buffalo, New York, Rochester, Schenectady, and Syracuse.
North Carolina—Charlotte and Greensboro.
North Dakota—Fargo.
Ohio—Akron, Cincinnati, Cleveland, Columbus, Dayton, Springfield, and Toledo.
Oklahoma—Oklahoma City and Tulsa.
Oregon—Portland.
Pennsylvania—Harrisburg, Philadelphia, Pittsburgh, and Scranton.
Rhode Island—Providence.
South Carolina—Charleston.
South Dakota—Sioux Falls.
Tennessee—Chattanooga, Memphis, and Nashville.
Texas—Austin, Dallas, Houston, and San Antonio.
Utah—Salt Lake City.
Vermont—Burlington.
Virginia—Norfolk and Richmond.
Washington—Seattle and Spokane.
West Virginia—Charleston and Wheeling.
Wisconsin—Madison and Milwaukee.
Wyoming—Cheyenne.

The *Zeppelin* stamps were withdrawn from sale in the above post offices on June 7, 1930, but the stamps were continued on sale in the Philatelic Agency for the benefit of stamp collectors until June 30, 1930.

NEW SERIES OF POSTAGE DUE STAMPS—ISSUE OF 1930

The new series of postage-due stamps was made available for issuance on post-masters' requisitions beginning July 1, 1930, replacing the 1894 series. Due stamps of the following denominations were included: ½-cent, 1-cent, 2-cent, 3-cent, 5-cent, 10-cent, 30-cent, 50-cent, $1, and $5.

The stamps are rectangular in shape, about $^{75}/_{100}$ by $^{87}/_{100}$ inch in size, and printed in red. The design for the first eight denominations (½ cent to 50 cents, inclusive) is identical except for the necessary change in numerals representing the value. A different design was used for the $1 and $5 denominations, which are horizontal.

The stamps of the ½-cent to 50-cent denominations are described as follows: Across the top of the stamps are the words "United States" and directly beneath in a curved panel are the words "Postage due" in white Roman letters. At the bottom of the stamps is the word "Cent" or "Cents", and in both lower corners within ovals with dark backgrounds, appear the white numerals indicating the denomination. In the center of the stamps appears a larger numeral or numerals, resting upon a background of lathe work. In the upper portion of the stamp, and on either side, are small triangular ornaments.

The $1 and $5 denominations have the same wording, except that the word "Dollar" or "Dollars" appears at the bottom of the stamp and the white numeral representing the value is within circles with dark backgrounds in both lower corners. In the center of these stamps, within a small panel, is the word "One" or "Five" in white Roman letters resting across a "$" mark with a background of ornamental lathe work. Triangular ornaments also appear in the upper portion of these stamps.

NEW 4-CENT ORDINARY POSTAGE STAMP, PORTRAIT OF TAFT— ISSUE OF 1930

Following the death of William Howard Taft, the department authorized the issuance of a new 4-cent ordinary postage stamp bearing his likeness. This stamp replaced the current stamp of the same denomination bearing the portrait of Martha Washington.

The central design is a portrait of the former President and late Chief Justice, with an open background. The name "Taft" appears on a ribbon scroll directly beneath the portrait. No change was made in the border design or in the color, which continued in brown.

The new stamp was first placed on sale June 4, 1930, at Cincinnati, Ohio, the former home of the subject of the stamp.

BATTLE OF BRADDOCK COMMEMORATIVE STAMP (2-CENT)—ISSUE OF 1930

This special issue of 2-cent stamps commemorates the one hundred and seventy-fifth anniversary of the Battle of Braddock.

The stamp is the same shape and size as the regular issue, $^{75}/_{100}$ by $^{87}/_{100}$ inch, and is printed in red ink. In a straight line across the top of the stamp are the words "United States postage" in white Roman letters and directly beneath is a semicircular panel bearing the words "Battle of Braddock's Field." This panel is supported on either side by acanthus scrolls. In both lower corners within ovals with dark backgrounds appears the white numeral "2." These ovals are connected by a panel bearing the word "Cents" in white Roman letters.

The central design is a statue of Col. George Washington with the years "1755" and "1930" in white numerals on either side, and directly beneath the statue in a small panel are the words "Colonel George Washington" in white Gothic letters. Ornamental triangles appear on either side in the upper portion of the stamp.

This new stamp was first placed on sale July 9, 1930, at Braddock, Pa.

GENERAL VON STEUBEN COMMEMORATIVE STAMP (2-CENT)— ISSUE OF 1930

  This special stamp was issued in commemoration of the two hundredth anniversary of the birth of General Von Steuben and in recognition of the exceptional services rendered the Colonial cause during the Revolutionary War in drilling and organizing the army.

  The stamp conforms in shape and size to the regular issue and is printed in red ink. Across the top of the stamp, arranged in two lines in a curved panel, are the words "United States postage" in white Roman letters. Extending below the panel is a vertically striped background, the upper border of which is composed of narrow acanthus scrolls.

  In both lower corners in circles with dark backgrounds appears the white numeral "2." In a dark panel connecting the circles is the word "Cents" in white Roman letters. Arising from each circle on the right and left is an acanthus leaf scroll which lends support to the large circular medallion in the central portion of the stamp bearing the raised head and bust of Von Steuben modeled from a medal. In a semicircle along the upper edge of the central medallion is the wording "1730—General Von Steuben—1930" in Roman type.

  This new stamp was first placed on sale September 17, 1930, at New York, N. Y.

CHANGE IN DESIGN OF 1½-CENT POSTAGE STAMP, PORTRAIT OF HARDING—ISSUE OF 1930

  This new issue of 1½-cent stamps contains a full-face likeness of the late President in lieu of the profile view originally used on this denomination. The border design of the new stamp was also changed to agree with the other stamps of the regular issue, series of 1922–23. The new stamp is of the same size as the regular issue and printed in brown ink.

  The central design on the 1½-cent stamp was reengraved in order to provide a more satisfactory likeness of the late President and to have the stamp conform in general style and quality of workmanship with the other stamps of the presidential series.

  The new 1½-cent Harding stamp was first placed on sale, in sheets and sidewise coils, at the post office in Marion, Ohio, on December 1, 1930.

GENERAL PULASKI COMMEMORATIVE STAMP (2-CENT)—ISSUE OF 1931

This special 2-cent commemorative postage stamp in honor of Gen. Casimir Pulaski was issued in recognition of the one hundred and fiftieth anniversary of the death of the noted Polish patriot and hero of the American Revolution. The stamp is the same shape and size as the regular issue, $75/100$ by $87/100$ inch in dimension, and is printed in red ink. The stamp has a flat, dark border with beveled outer edge, slightly indented at the sides. On the border at the top in two lines is the wording "United States postage", in white-faced Roman letters. In both lower corners in white bordered circles is the numeral "2" in white-faced Roman and above the circles in the bordering panel in white numerals are the dates, "1748" at the left and "1779" at the right, representing the dates of birth and death, respectively, of General Pulaski. Across the bottom of the stamp in a dark panel with white edges connecting the numerals is the word "Cents" in white Roman lettering. In a central panel of oval form with a narrow white edge is the likeness of General Pulaski modeled from a portrait in Jones's History of Georgia, printed from an etching by H. B. Hall in 1871. In a white curved ribbon panel at the base of the portrait are the words "General Pulaski" in red Gothic letters. Projecting from behind the central panel with their staffs extending to the upper corners are the flags of the two nations, that of the United States to the left and the Republic of Poland to the right.

The General Pulaski commemorative stamp was first placed on sale January 16, 1931, at the following post offices:

Savannah, Ga.	Detroit, Mich.	Cleveland, Ohio.
Chicago, Ill.	Brooklyn, N. Y.	Toledo, Ohio.
Gary, Ind.	Buffalo, N. Y.	Pittsburgh, Pa.
South Bend, Ind.	New York, N. Y.	Milwaukee, Wis.

RED CROSS COMMEMORATIVE POSTAGE STAMP (2-CENT)—ISSUE OF 1931

This stamp was issued to commemorate the fiftieth anniversary of the founding of the American Red Cross.

The stamp is printed in two colors, black and red, and is the same size as the regular issue, $75/100$ by $87/100$ inch, arranged as an upright rectangle. The stamp is inclosed in a border formed by a heavy black outer and lighter inner line slightly indented along the center on all four sides. Across the top of the stamp in two lines are the words "United States postage" in white-faced Roman lettering. The central design of the stamp, printed in black, is the figure of a Red Cross nurse kneeling before the globe with outstretched hands, reproduced from the 1930 poster entitled "The Greatest Mother." In the upper part of the stamp at the left of the figure is the Greek cross with five equal squares, the emblem of the organization, printed in red. Arranged vertically, opposite the indentation on either side, are the dates in black Gothic figures

"1881" at the left and "1931" at the right. In both lower corners within white bordered ovals with black background appears the white numeral "2." The ovals are surmounted by acanthus scroll ornaments. Across the bottom of the stamp in a straight line between the ovals containing the denomination numeral is the word "Cents" in white Roman letters.

The Red Cross commemorative stamp was placed on sale May 21, 1931, at Washington, D. C., national headquarters of the American Red Cross, and Dansville, N. Y., where the first local chapter was established.

YORKTOWN COMMEMORATIVE POSTAGE STAMP (2-CENT)—ISSUE OF 1931

The Battle of Yorktown stamp commemorates the one hundred and fiftieth anniversary of the surrender of Cornwallis.

The stamp is rectangular in shape, $^{89}/_{100}$ by $1^{46}/_{100}$ inches in dimension. It is printed in two colors, the background being in red, and the three portraits composing the central design in black. In a horizontal line across the top of the stamp are the words "United States postage" in small white Roman letters. Directly below on a white ribbon panel in red lettering is the word "Yorktown" in the center with the dates on either side, "1781" at the left and "1931" at the right. At the base of the stamp in a small panel with curled scrolls at either end is the word "Cents" in white-faced Roman on a solid background. In each lower corner in a small panel with narrow white border and scrolled top is the numeral "2" in white Roman on a solid background. Extending across the center of the stamp are three ovals with white outer and red inner line borders containing, in order, beginning at the left, the portraits of Rochambeau, Washington, and De Grasse, the names appearing in red lettering on white ribbon panels at the base of the ovals.

The Yorktown stamp was first placed on sale October 19, 1931, at the post offices in Yorktown, Va., and Wethersfield, Conn. (branch of Hartford). The latter post office was included in the first day list for the reason that it was at that place the plans for the Yorktown campaign were agreed to by General Washington and Count Rochambeau.

WASHINGTON BICENTENNIAL COMMEMORATIVE POSTAGE STAMPS (½-CENT TO 10-CENT, INCLUSIVE)—ISSUE OF 1932

In cooperation with the national celebration of the two hundredth anniversary of the birth of George Washington, the department authorized a special series of 12 postage stamps in denominations of ½ cent to 10 cents, inclusive, to be kept on sale in post offces throughout the anniversary period in lieu of the regular series of stamps.

The stamps are of regulation size, $^{75}/_{100}$ by $^{87}/_{100}$ inch in dimension, arranged vertically, and have as the central designs portraits of Washington modeled from the works of noted artists. The stamps are described as follows:

One-half cent.—The stamp is dark brown in color and has a flat paneled border with darker interior over which is laid a circular panel in which appears the likeness of Washington taken from a miniature painted by Charles Wilson Peale in 1777, the original of which is in the Metropolitan Museum of Art. The central design is bordered by white inner and outer lines forming a narrow circular panel, within which, across the top, is the legend "United States postage" in white-faced Roman, the remainder being filled in with laurel leaves. The circular panel is overlaid and supported at the base by a curved white ribbon containing the dates "1732" at the left and "1932" at the right, with the word "Washington" underneath across the center of the ribbon. In each lower corner within a white edged circular panel is the fractional numeral "½" in white Roman on a dark background. The circles are connected by a horizontal panel containing the word "Cent" in white Roman letters.

One-cent.—The stamp is printed in green. Across the top is a flat panel containing, in two horizontal lines, the words "United States postage" in white-faced Roman. The panel is supported at either end by vertical flat fluted columns, the bases of which extend to the bottom of the stamp and hold in each lower corner a white edged oval panel inclosing the numeral "1" in white Roman on a dark background. In the center of the stamp slightly overlapping the side columns is a large oval with dark background and white line border containing a reproduction of the profile bust of Washington by Jean Antoine Houdon made in 1785 and now in Mount Vernon. Across the base of the oval is a white-ribbon panel containing in dark Gothic lettering the name "Washington" in the center and the dates "1732" at the left and "1932" at the right. In a horizontal line across the base of the stamp is the word "Cent" in white Roman on a dark background.

One-and-one-half cent.—The stamp is light brown in color with a narrow white border within which in the upper part is a flat tinted panel inclosing a background of darker shade. Extending to the top of the stamp is a semicircular panel with white edges and dark ground, resting at either end on fluted side columns which rise slightly above midway of the stamp. Within this panel appear the words "United States postage" in white-faced Roman. At the base of the column in each lower corner is a small rectangular panel with beveled upper corners containing the figures "1½" in white-faced Roman on a solid ground. The small panels are connected by a horizontal panel with dark ground, containing the word "Cents" in white Roman. In the space under the arch in the central part of the stamp is a likeness of Washington modeled from a painting known as the Virginia Colonel made at Mount Vernon in 1772 by Charles Wilson Peale, the original of which is now in Washington and Lee University. At the base of the portrait is a white-ribbon panel containing the word "Washington" in the center and the dates "1732" at the left and "1932" at the right in the curved ends which extend slightly upward and overlap the lower ends of the side columns.

Two-cent.—The stamp is printed in red and is inclosed in a narrow white-line border with small ornaments resembling fleurs-de-lis in each upper corner. Beginning slightly above the center on either side and reaching the top is a semicircular panel with the words "United States postage" in white Roman on a solid background. The ends of the panel are supported by acanthus scrolls rising from upright ovals in each lower corner. Within these ovals with white edges is the Roman numeral "2" in white on a solid background. At the base of the stamp between the ovals is a white bordered panel with the word "Cents" in white Roman letters on a solid background. In the center of the stamp with a dark background is the likeness of Washington by Gilbert Stuart from a painting made at Germantown, Pa., in 1796, known as the Atheneum portrait, the original of which is now in the Boston Museum of Fine Arts. On a white ribbon below the portrait is the name "Washington" in dark Roman lettering. On the raised ends of the ribbon are the dates "1732" at the left and "1932" at the right.

Three-cent.—The stamp is printed in purple ink and is inclosed in a white-line border. In a curved panel having white edges and solid background across the top of the stamp are the words "United States postage" in white Roman letters. The panel is supported at each end by small acanthus scrolls. In each upper corner of the stamp is a small sunken triangle. In each lower corner is a circle with white edge inclosing the white Roman numeral "3" on a dark background. Across the bottom of the stamp connecting the circles is a narrow panel containing the word "Cents" in white Roman on a solid background. Above the panel is a ribbon with the name "Washington" in small dark Roman lettering. On the ends of the ribbon, which are curved upward to rest over the circles, are the dates "1732" at the left and "1932" at the right. In the central part of the stamp is the likeness of Washington in the uniform of a general with cocked hat reproduced from a portrait by Charles Wilson Peale painted at Valley Forge in 1777. The original portrait is now in the State Normal School at West Chester, Pa.

Four-cent.—The stamp is printed in warm brown and has a narrow rectangular border indented at the sides and ends. Across the top of the stamp in a narrow double-curved, white-edged panel are the words "United States postage" in two lines in white Roman letters on solid background. The panel is widened at the center to accommodate the last word, and the ends of the widened portion are supported by acanthus scrolls which rise from each side of the large oval occupying the central part of the stamp. Within the large oval is the likeness of Washington taken from a painting by Charles Peale Polk, now in the possession of Mr. William Patten, Rhinebeck, N. Y. Below the portrait in a curved white ribbon in dark Gothic lettering is the name "Washington" in the center and the dates "1732" at the left and "1932" at the right. In each lower corner is a circular panel with dark ground and white edge with the numeral "4" in white Roman. Between the circles in a narrow white bordered panel curved to conform with the ribbon above is the word "Cents" in white Roman letters.

Five-cent.—The stamp, printed in blue, is bordered by a beveled edge panel indented at the sides and ends. Across the top in a double curve in white Roman letters are the words "United States postage" in two lines. On each side of the word "Postage" is a small acanthus scroll. In the center of the stamp is a large dark shield with white-line border containing the likeness of Washington from a painting by Charles Wilson Peale made in 1795, and now in the possession of the New York Historical Society. On a curved ribbon below the portrait are the dates "1732" at the left and "1932" at the right, and the name "Washington" in the center in dark Gothic lettering. In each lower corner is a rectangular shaped panel containing the numeral "5" in white Roman with dark background.

Six-cent.—The stamp is printed in orange color. The stamp is inclosed by a rectangular panel with white edge forming a frame for the central design representing Washington in the uniform of a general reproduced from a painting by John Trumbull in 1792, now in Yale University. Over the head is a narrow semicircular panel with white-line border and solid background extending, at the center, to the top of the stamp. Within this panel are the words "United States postage" in white Roman letters on a solid background. The panel is supported on each side by small acanthus scrolls. In each upper corner is a triangular sunken panel with white edge and darker interior. In each lower corner is an upright oval with white edge containing the numeral "6" in white Roman on a solid background. At the base in a horizontal line between the ovals is the word "Cents" in white Roman. Under the portrait is a curved white ribbon bearing in the center the name "Washington" in dark Roman lettering. On the ends of the ribbon, which rest at the top of the ovals on each side, are the dates "1732" at the left and "1932" at the right.

Seven-cent.—The stamp is printed in black ink with white edge and gray paneled border on the sides and top. The upright panels are slightly indented at the sides. Inside the border is a background of darker gray. Along the upper edge of the stamp in a horizontal line are the words "United States postage" in white Roman. In each lower corner is a circle with white edge and black ground inclosing the numeral "7" in white Roman. The circles are connected by a white edged panel containing the word "Cents" in white Roman on a dark background. In the center of the stamp is a large oval with light background and white border which contains a likeness of Washington in a colonial uniform showing the head and bust reproduced from a full length portrait painted by John Trumbull in 1780, the original of which is now in the Metropolitan Museum of Art. Below the portrait is a double curved white ribbon bearing in the center in black Roman lettering the name "Washington." On the raised ends of the ribbon are the dates "1732" at the left and "1932" at the right.

Eight-cent.—The stamp is of olive green color and is inclosed in a white-line border. In a large upright oval in the center of the stamp is a profile bust portrait of Washington facing to the left, reproduced from a crayon drawing made from life by Charles B. J. F. Saint Memin at Philadelphia in 1798. Inclosing the central oval is a narrow panel with white edges and dark ground containing the inscription "United States postage" in white Roman letters. On each side of the central oval near the top is shown the upper corner of a shieldlike inner panel. In each lower corner in an upright rectangular panel with white edge and double curved top is the numeral "8" on a dark background. At the base of the stamp in a narrow white edged panel between the numerals is the word "Cents" in white Roman on a dark background. At the base of the central oval is a white ribbon with the name "Washington" in dark lettering in the center and on the curved and raised ends the dates "1732" at the left and "1932" at the right.

Nine-cent.—The stamp is printed in salmon pink with a white-line border. At the center in a large panel rectangular in shape below, oval and slightly widened in the upper portion, is the likeness of Washington modeled from a pastel portrait in the possession of the Masonic lodge of Alexandria, Va., for whom it was drawn from life by W. Williams in 1794. Above the central panel in a double curved white ribbon with scrolled ends are the words "United States postage" in dark Roman. In each lower corner of the stamp is the numeral "9" in white Roman. In a horizontal line at the base between the numerals is the word "Cents" in white Roman. On a white ribbon at the base of the portrait within the central panel is the name "Washington" in dark Roman. In the curved ends of the ribbon above the numerals are the dates "1732" at the left and "1932" at the right. Rising from each ribbon end is a small laurel branch.

Ten-cent.—The stamp is yellow in color. The sides and top are slightly indented along the center and are bordered by a narrow panel having dark center and white edges. In the upper part, overlapping the border at the top and sides is a narrow white edged panel with double curve and small acanthus scrolls at each end containing in two lines the words "United States postage" in white Roman letters on a dark background. The panel is widened at the center to provide space for "Postage." In the center of the stamp is a large oval with white edge and dark ground inclosing the portrait of Washington taken from a painting by Gilbert Stuart in 1795, now in the possession of the Metropolitan Museum of Art in New York City. Within the oval under the portrait is a narrow curved panel with white edge and dark ground containing in Gothic lettering the name "Washington" in the center and the dates on each side, "1732" at the left and "1932" at the right. In each lower corner is a white edged panel, slightly shield-shaped on the bottom line, in which appears the numeral "10" in white Roman on a dark background. At the base of the stamp in a horizontal line is the word "Cents" in white Roman letters on a dark background.

The bicentennial stamps were first placed on sale January 1, 1932, at the post office in Washington, D. C.

III OLYMPIC WINTER GAMES COMMEMORATIVE STAMP (2-CENT)— ISSUE OF 1932

This special stamp was issued in honor of the International Olympic Winter Games held at Lake Placid, N. Y., in February, 1932.

The stamp is a horizontal rectangle $^{75}/_{100}$ by $^{87}/_{100}$ inch in dimension, printed in red ink and inclosed in a single-line border. Across the top of the stamp in a straight line are the words "United States postage" in white Roman, and directly below in white lettering is the wording "III Olympic Winter Games."

The central design is a representation of a ski jumper in action, in the position of descent from right to left, with a background formed by a snow-covered mountain landscape and overcast sky. Across the base of the central design in two lines in dark Gothic lettering appear the wording "Lake Placid, New York", and the dates "February 4–13, 1932." In each lower corner is a large white numeral "2." Extending across the bottom of the stamp between the numerals are the words "Two cents" in white Roman.

The new commemorative stamp was first placed on sale at the post office in Lake Placid, N. Y., on January 25, 1932.

ARBOR DAY COMMEMORATIVE POSTAGE STAMP (2-CENT)—ISSUE OF 1932

This stamp was authorized in commemoration of the sixtieth anniversary of the establishment of Arbor Day, on April 22, 1932, and in honor of the one hundredth anniversary of the birth of J. Sterling Morton, through whose efforts a day was first officially set aside for the planting of trees by the State of Nebraska in 1872.

The stamp is of the same size as the regular issue, $^{75}/_{100}$ by $^{87}/_{100}$ inch in dimension, printed in red ink. It is surrounded by a narrow white-line border within which on either side rises a large tree with spreading branches that meet at the top in the form of an arbor. Across the top of the stamp in two curved lines are the words "United States postage" in white Roman. In a curved line inside the arch are the words "Arbor Day" in red Roman. Across the bottom of the stamp in a narrow panel, with solid background and white edges, are the words "Two cents" in white Roman. Directly above the panel on each side within a circle with white edge and solid background is the large numeral "2." Acanthus scrolls extend from the tops of the circles over the base of the trees. The central design of the stamp pictures the planting of a tree by a girl and boy, the former holding the tree in position while the earth is filled in by the boy. In the left background is a small house with forest trees extending to the right. In a straight line below the central figures are the dates "1872–1932", in white Roman.

The Arbor Day stamp was first placed on sale in Nebraska City, Nebr., the former home of J. Sterling Morton, on April 22, 1932.

XTH OLYMPIAD COMMEMORATIVE STAMPS (3-CENT AND 5-CENT)— ISSUE OF 1932

This special series of postage stamps in the 3-cent and 5-cent denominations was issued in recognition of the International Olympic games held at Los Angeles, Calif., from July 30 to August 14, 1932.

The two stamps are of the regular size, $^{75}/_{100}$ by $^{87}/_{100}$ inch in dimension, and are identical in every detail except as to color, denomination numerals, and central subject.

The 3-cent stamp is printed in purple ink and has for the central design the likeness of an Olympic runner in crouched position as if ready for the starting signal. The 5-cent stamp is printed in blue and includes as the central subject a representation of the Roman discus thrower modeled from the statue "Discobolus", back of which on a solid background is an outline of the globe with the lower part obscured by clouds.

The central subjects are in oval panels bordered along the top and sides with a narrow panel in the shape of a horseshoe with open part below. Within the bordering panels, which have white edges and solid backgrounds, is the inscription "Xth Olympiad—Los Angeles, 1932" in white Roman. Across the top of the stamps in a narrow white edged panel with solid background are the words "United States postage" in white Roman letters. Within a circular panel with white edge and solid ground in each lower corner is the large numeral "3" or "5", conforming to the denomination of the stamp. Rising from the top of each circle is an acanthus leaf which overlaps the base of the horseshoe panel. Connecting the circles containing the numerals and forming the base of the stamp is a narrow panel, with solid background and white edges, containing the word "Cents" in white Roman. On either side from behind the upper part of the horseshoe panel rises a smoking torch.

The Olympic games stamps were first placed on sale at the post office in Los Angeles, Calif., on June 15, 1932.

ORDINARY POSTAGE STAMP (3-CENT)—ISSUE OF 1932

The issuance of this new design 3-cent stamp containing as the central subject the likeness of Washington reproduced from the Stuart portrait was authorized after the enactment of legislation increasing the postage rate on letter mail of the first class, effective July 6, 1932, to conform to the established policy of having the likeness of the First President on the stamp representing the initial rate of postage for such mail matter.

The stamp is identical in size and design to the 2-cent stamp of the Washington Bicentennial series except for the change in denomination numeral and omission of the dates. The stamp is printed in purple ink.

The new 3-cent stamp was first placed on sale on June 16, 1932, at the post office in Washington, D. C.

STAMP COILS (6-CENT)—ISSUE OF 1932

To meet the public demand under the new postage rates, effective July 6, 1932, the department authorized the issuance of 6-cent stamps in coils of 500 and 1,000 each.

The stamps in the coils are of the same design as the 6-cent stamp of the regular series, containing the likeness of Garfield and printed in orange color.

The new 6-cent coil was first placed on sale on August 18, 1932, at Los Angeles, Calif., in connection with the National Philatelic Exhibition and American Philatelic Society Convention, held August 15 to 20, 1932.

AIR-MAIL STAMP (8-CENT)—ISSUE OF 1932

The issuance of an air-mail stamp in this denomination was required to conform to the new air-mail rate which became effective July 6, 1932.

The 8-cent air-mail stamp is of the same size, shape, and design as the 5-cent air-mail stamp of the current issue, containing a reproduction of the insignia of the air-mail service as the central design. No modification was made except to substitute the denomination numeral "8" in the circular panel in each lower corner and to change the color to olive green.

The 8-cent air-mail stamp was first placed on sale in Washington, D. C., on September 26, 1932.

WILLIAM PENN COMMEMORATIVE STAMP (3-CENT)—ISSUE OF 1932

This stamp was issued to commemorate the two hundred and fiftieth anniversary of the arrival of William Penn in America.

The stamp is of the same size and shape as the stamps of the regular issue, $75/100$ by $87/100$ inch in dimension, and is printed in purple ink. In a horizontal line across the top of the stamp are the words "United States postage" in small solid Roman letters. In the center of the stamp is the likeness of William Penn in armor, reproduced from an engraving of a portrait painted from life in 1666, the original of which is in the possession of the Pennsylvania Historical Society. On either side of the head, running perpendicularly, are the dates "1682", the year of William Penn's arrival in America, at the left, and "1932" at the right. Within an upright rectangle with white edges and solid background, in each lower corner, is a white keystone bearing the numeral "3" in solid Gothic. In a narrow panel across the base connecting the corner rectangles is the word "Cents" in white Gothic. Below the portrait on a narrow white ribbon panel is the name "William Penn" in small solid Gothic letters.

The William Penn commemorative stamp was first placed on sale October 24, 1932, at the post offices in New Castle, Del., Chester, Pa., and Philadelphia, Pa.

DANIEL WEBSTER COMMEMORATIVE STAMP (3-CENT)—ISSUE OF 1932

This stamp was authorized in honor of the one hundred and fiftieth anniversary of the birth of Daniel Webster.

The stamp is the same size as the regular issue, $75/100$ by $87/100$ inch in dimension. The stamp is of the 3-cent denomination, printed in purple. The central subject is a full-face likeness of Daniel Webster, reproduced from a marble bust by Daniel Chester French at Franklin, N. H., the birthplace of Webster. In a semicircular white ribbon panel, with folded ends, over the portrait and touching the border at top and sides are the words "United States postage" in small solid Roman letters. In an upright oval panel with white edge and solid background in each lower corner is the numeral "3" in white Roman. In a panel with solid background, connecting the ovals, is the word "Cents" in white Roman. Above the base panel is a narrow ribbon with folded ends which extend over the ovals containing the denomination numerals. In the center of this ribbon at the base of the portrait are the words "Daniel Webster" in dark Roman letters, and in the folded ends are the dates "1782" at the left and "1932" at the right. On each side, extending from the top of the stamp to the ovals in the lower corners and partially obscured by the end of the semicircular panel, is a fasces. The stamp is inclosed in a narrow white-line border.

The Daniel Webster commemorative stamp was first placed on sale October 24, 1932, at Exeter, Franklin, and Hanover, N. H.

GENERAL OGLETHORPE COMMEMORATIVE STAMP (3-CENT)— ISSUE OF 1933

This special issue of postage stamps was authorized to commemorate the two hundredth anniversary of the settlement of Georgia, and in honor of General Oglethorpe, the founder of the colony.

The stamp is of the same size as the regular issue, $75/100$ by $87/100$ inch in dimension, without border, and is printed in purple ink. In a horizontal line across the top of the stamp in shaded Roman letters are the words "United States postage." The central subject of the stamp is the likeness of General Oglethorpe, wearing a coat of armor. In each lower corner, within an upright rectangular panel with tinted face and narrow white-line border, is the large numeral "3" in white Roman. In a narrow panel at the bottom of the stamp is the word "Cents" in white Roman. On a white panel directly above the base panel is the name "General Oglethorpe" in dark Gothic letters. On each side of the head, arranged perpendicularly, are the dates "1733" at the left and "1933" at the right.

The General Oglethorpe commemorative stamp was first placed on sale February 12, 1933, at the post office in Savannah, Ga.

PROCLAMATION OF PEACE COMMEMORATIVE STAMP (3-CENT)—
ISSUE OF 1933

This special stamp commemorates the one hundred and fiftieth anniversary of the issuance by General Washington of the official order containing the proclamation of peace, marking, officially, the ending of hostilities in the war for independence.

The stamp is the same size as the regular issue, $75/100$ by $87/100$ inch in dimension. The stamp is inclosed in a narrow double-line border and is printed in purple ink. At the top of the stamp in a narrow panel with solid background and ornamental ends are the words "U. S. postage" in white Roman. Underneath this panel in three lines is the inscription "Washington's Headquarters, Newburgh, N. Y., 1783–1933" in small dark Gothic lettering. The central design is a representation of the Hasbrouck House at Newburgh, N. Y., used as headquarters by General Washington at the time the proclamation was issued. The Hudson River is pictured at the left of the house and in the background are ranges of hills following the course of the river. In the lower right corner of the central design is a large tree with rocks and plants around the base. In the opposite lower corner is a cannon partly hidden by shrubbery. In front and to the left of the house is a staff bearing a flag representing the first Stars and Stripes. The large numeral "3" in dark Gothic is inclosed within a shield-shaped panel with light background at the center of the lower edge. On each side of the panel containing the denomination numeral is a ribbon with folded ends bearing the words "Three" at the left and "Cents" at the right.

The Proclamation of Peace commemorative stamp was first placed on sale April 19, 1933, at the post office in Newburgh, N. Y.

CHICAGO CENTURY OF PROGRESS EXPOSITION COMMEMORATIVE
STAMPS (1-CENT AND 3-CENT)—ISSUE OF 1933

This special issue of stamps commemorates the Century of Progress International Exposition held in Chicago, Ill., beginning June 1, 1933.

The stamps are of the same size as the regular issue, $75/100$ by $87/100$ inch in dimension, arranged horizontally. Both stamps are inclosed in narrow double-line borders. The 1-cent stamp is printed in green and the 3-cent stamp in purple.

The central design of the 1-cent stamp depicts old Fort Dearborn, pioneer outpost at Chicago, as restored in 1816. A blockhouse of the old fort appears in the foreground, partly overshadowed below and with a stockade fence extending from each side to the edge of the stamp. In the background are trees and other buildings of the fort. In a short ribbon panel at the top of the stamp are the words "U. S. postage" in solid Gothic. On each side opposite the lower edge of this panel are the dates "1833" at the left and "1933" at the right. Above the blockhouse in a curved line are the words "Chicago Century of Progress" in solid Gothic. In each lower corner is a circular panel with light ground and double-line border inclosing the denomination numeral "I" in solid

Roman. In a narrow panel with curved ends and solid background at the base of the stamp is the word "Cent" in white Roman. Above the base panel in solid block lettering are the words "Fort Dearborn."

The 3-cent stamp has for a central design a reproduction of the Federal building, with its three massive towers, on the exposition grounds. In a short narrow panel with solid background and white border at the top of the stamp are the words "U. S. postage" in white Roman. Below this top panel and on each side of the upper part of the central tower are the inscriptions "Century of Progress" at the left and "Chicago 1833–1933" at the right in solid Gothic lettering arranged in two lines. In a horizontal line at the base of the central design are the words "Federal Building" in small solid block letters and directly underneath is the word "Cents" in white Roman. Within a circular panel with white border and solid background in each lower corner is the white Roman numeral "III."

The Century of Progress commemorative stamps were first placed on sale May 25, 1933, at the main post office in Chicago, Ill.

SOUVENIR SHEETS OF CENTURY OF PROGRESS COMMEMORATIVE STAMPS—ISSUE OF 1933

This special issue of 1-cent and 3-cent postage stamps of the Century of Progress design in sheets of 25 stamps each was authorized for printing on the stamp press included in the Government exhibit at the Chicago Century of Progress Exposition.

The sheets are approximately 4¾ by 5⅝ inches in dimension, and are ungummed and without perforations. In narrow margins on the four sides of the sheets in small Gothic lettering, corresponding to the color of the denomination, is the following wording: "Printed by the Treasury Department, Bureau of Engraving and Printing, under authority of James A. Farley, Postmaster General, at a Century of Progress. In compliment to the American Philatelic Society for its convention and exhibition, Chicago, Illinois, August 1933."

The special sheets of Century of Progress stamps were first placed on sale August 25, 1933, at the philatelic station, Chicago, Ill., operated in connection with the annual convention of the American Philatelic Society, held at the Medinah Michigan Avenue Club, Chicago, August 21–26. The stamps were also placed on sale August 28, 1933, at Chicago Century of Progress Postal Station, Exposition Grounds, for the convenience of visitors.

Stamps of this special printing were not placed on sale at other post offices. They were, however, placed on sale August 28, 1933, at the Philatelic Agency, Post Office Department, for the benefit of stamp collectors.

N. R. A. EMERGENCY POSTAGE STAMP (3-CENT)—ISSUE OF 1933

This special issue of postage stamps was authorized by the Department to direct attention to and arouse the support of the Nation in the National Recovery Act.

The stamp is of the same size as the regular issue, $^{75}/_{100}$ by $^{87}/_{100}$ inch, and is surrounded by a narrow double-line border. The stamp is arranged horizontally and is printed in purple ink. At the top of the stamp in dark Roman lettering are the words "U. S. postage."

The principal design, spaced slightly to the right of the center of the stamp, contains figures representing a farmer, a business man, an industrial worker, and a woman employee. Rays of light, as from the rising sun, extend from the upper right corner toward the central group. In the upper part of the space, between the central subject and the left margin, in dark

Gothic letters, are the words "Three cents", arranged in two lines, and some distance below, in dark Gothic letters of larger size, is the abbreviation "N. R. A." The denomination is designated by "3¢" within a circle with white background in the lower left corner of the stamp. In a horizontal line along the bottom of the stamp, in small Gothic lettering, are the words "In a common determination."

The N. R. A. stamp was first placed on sale August 15, 1933, at Washington, D. C.

GENERAL KOSCIUSKO COMMEMORATIVE POSTAGE STAMP
(5-CENT)—ISSUE OF 1933

U.S. POSTAGE
FIVE CENTS
KOŚCIUSZKO
1783
1933
5¢

The stamp in honor of Gen. Thaddeus Kosciusko was issued in connection with the one hundred and fiftieth anniversary of his naturalization as an American citizen.

The stamp is of the regulation size, $^{75}/_{100}$ by $^{87}/_{100}$ inch, printed in blue. Surrounding the stamp is a narrow panel ruled diagonally, bordered by a single inner line with double lines along the outer margin. The likeness of General Kosciusko, modeled from a statue in Lafayette Park, Washington, D. C., appears at the right of the center with the top of the pedestal base resting in the lower right corner. In a horizontal line in the upper left portion of the stamp are the words "U. S. postage" in dark Roman. Immediately below this inscription are the words "Five cents" in solid Gothic lettering, beneath which is a scroll-like ornament. In the space below is the name "Kosciuszko" in solid Gothic with the dates "1783" and "1933", directly below, arranged in two lines. The denomination designation, "5¢", is enclosed in a circular panel with light ground in the lower left corner, behind which is shown a group of trees.

The Kosciusko stamp was first placed on sale October 13, 1933, at Chicago, Ill., Boston, Mass., Detroit, Mich., Kosciusko, Miss., St. Louis, Mo., Buffalo, N. Y., and Pittsburgh, Pa.

SPECIAL "GRAF ZEPPELIN" AIR MAIL STAMP (50-CENT)—ISSUE OF
1933

UNITED STATES POSTAGE
A CENTURY OF PROGRESS FLIGHT
50¢

This special stamp was provided for use on air mail matter carried on the flight of the *Graf Zeppelin* to the Century of Progress Exposition, in October 1933.

The stamp is the same shape and size as the current air mail stamp, $^{75}/_{100}$ by $1^{84}/_{100}$ inches. The central design is a representation of the *Graf Zeppelin* over the Atlantic Ocean. To the right appears the hangar at Friedrichshafen, and to the left is shown the Federal Building at the Century of Progress Exposition. Across the top of the stamp appear the words: "United States postage", in solid Roman letters, and immediately underneath are the words "A Century of Progress Flight" in smaller Gothic type. In a large oval with dark background

below the central design is the denomination designation "50¢" in white lettering. The stamp is enclosed in a border formed by two narrow parallel lines.

The special Zeppelin stamp was placed on sale at the following post offices
until after the completion of the flight: Miami, Fla., Chicago, Ill., New York,
N. Y., and Akron, Ohio. The stamp was first placed on sale at New York, N. Y.,
on October 2, 1933. The stamp was placed on sale in the Philatelic Agency,
Post Office Department, October 5, 1933.

LITTLE AMERICA POSTAGE STAMP (3-CENT)—ISSUE OF 1933

This stamp was issued for use on letters mailed through the Little America
post office, established at the base camp of the Byrd Antarctic Expedition, in
the territory of the South Pole.

The stamp is of the same size and shape as special-delivery stamps, $83/100$ by
$1^{42}/100$ inches, arranged vertically. The stamp is surrounded by a narrow double-
line border, and is printed in navy blue. Across the top of the stamp is the
inscription "Byrd Antarctic Expedition II", arranged in two lines in solid
Roman. In the central part of the stamp is a large geographic globe, the sides
of which are partly hidden behind the border. Routes of the several Byrd
flights are depicted by dotted lines, with the dates thereof in solid Gothic. Pro-
posed new flights to the Antarctic and to the South Pole are also indicated.
The position of the base camp is marked by a solid dark circle, with the wording "Little America" in solid Gothic extending parallel with the meridian to the
west of the base. Within a circle with white ground and double-line border,
in each lower corner, is the large numeral "3" in solid color. At the bottom
of the stamp is a narrow horizontal panel with white ground containing the
word "Cents" in solid Gothic. In a ribbon panel directly above, with white
ground, are the words "U. S. postage", also in solid Gothic lettering. A
clouded effect, heavy below and lighter at the top, forms a background for the
central globe.

Since the Department had no means of providing for the transportation of
this philatelic mail to Little America, other than through the facilities of the
Byrd Antarctic Expedition, arrangements were made with the expedition to
accept covers for mailing through the Little America post office, bearing appropriate postmark, at a service charge of 50 cents for each letter, exclusive of the
postage rate of 3 cents, to cover which the special stamp was issued. The Little
America stamp was first placed on sale October 9, 1933, at the Philatelic
Agency, Post Office Department. The stamp was not distributed to post offices
for sale to the public.

SOUVENIR SHEET OF LITTLE AMERICA STAMPS (3-CENT)—ISSUE OF 1934

These special sheets, each containing six Little America stamps, were authorized for printing on the postage-stamp press included in the display of the Bureau of Engraving and Printing at the National Stamp Exhibition of 1934 held at Rockefeller Center, New York, N. Y., February 10–18.

The special sheet is approximately 3⅞ by 3⅝ inches in dimension, ungummed and unperforated. The following printing appears in small type in blue ink on the four sides of the sheets: "Printed by the Treasury Department, Bureau of Engraving and Printing, under authority of James A. Farley, Postmaster General, New York, N. Y., February 10–18, 1934, in compliment to the National Stamp Exhibition of 1934."

The souvenir sheets of Little America stamps were first placed on sale February 10, 1934, at the branch Philatelic Agency operated in connection with the National Stamp Exhibition. In addition to these special sheets, the branch agency had available for sale stocks of the various commemorative stamps, from the William Penn issue to date.

To facilitate the dispatch of mail by visitors, a separate substation of the New York post office was established on the exhibition floor, for the use of which a special canceling stamp, reading as follows, was provided: "National Stamp Exhibition Sta., New York, N. Y." As the Little America stamp was issued primarily for use on mail dispatched on the Byrd Antarctic Expedition, the special sheets of this stamp, as described herein, were not issued to and sold through post offices.

For the benefit of stamp collectors who did not attend the National Stamp Exhibition, provision was made to place the souvenir sheets of Little America stamps on sale at the Philatelic Agency, Post Office Department, beginning February 19, 1934.

MARYLAND TERCENTENARY COMMEMORATIVE POSTAGE STAMP (3-CENT)—ISSUE OF 1934

This special issue of stamps was authorized to commemorate the three hundredth anniversary of the settlement of Maryland.

The stamp is of the same size and shape as the regular issue, $\frac{75}{100}$ by $\frac{87}{100}$ inch in dimension, arranged horizontally. It is inclosed in a narrow double-line border. Within a narrow panel across the top of the stamp is the wording "Maryland Tercentenary" in white Roman, on a solid background. In the widened ends of the panel are the dates "1634" at the left and "1934" at the right in white Gothic. The panel is supported by ornamental brackets at each end. The color of this stamp is red.

The central design is a representation of the two sailing vessels on which the first Maryland colony came to America. On a curved ribbon at the left of the central design is the inscription "The Ark and the Dove" in dark Old English lettering. In a corresponding position at the right is the Maryland coat of arms. Within circular panels with white borders and solid background in both lower corners is the large denomination numeral "3." Between the circles along the bottom of the stamp in a narrow panel with white edges and solid background and arranged in two lines is the wording "U. S. postage" and "Three cents."

The Maryland Tercentenary stamp was first placed on sale on March 23, 1934, at the post office in St. Marys City, Md where the first settlement was located.

COMMEMORATIVE POSTAGE STAMP IN HONOR OF MOTHERS
(3-CENT)—ISSUE OF 1934

This special stamp was issued as a tribute to the Mothers of America.

The stamp is in the form of a horizontal rectangle, $^{84}\!/_{100}$ by $1^{44}\!/_{100}$ inches in dimension, inclosed in a narrow double-line border. The color of the stamp is purple.

To the right of the center of the stamp facing the left is a reproduction of the painting by James Abbott McNeill Whistler, entitled "Portrait of My Mother." Along the top of the stamp at the left in solid Old English lettering are the words "U. S. postage." Directly below, arranged in four lines, in solid Gothic letters is the inscription "In Memory and in Honor of the Mothers of America." Underneath the inscription, in two lines, are the words "Three cents" in solid Gothic. In the lower left corner is a vase containing carnations.

The mothers' commemorative stamp was first placed on sale May 2, 1934, at Washington, D. C.

AIR-MAIL STAMP (6-CENT)—ISSUE OF 1934

The issuance of this new-denomination air-mail stamp was required to conform to the adjusted air-mail rates which became effective on July 1, 1934.

The 6-cent air-mail postage stamp is identical in size and design with the 8-cent air-mail stamp, the only alteration being that of the change in the denomination numeral to "6" and the color from olive-green to orange. The department did not authorize a first day of sale for this stamp, but it was available at many post offices on July 1, 1934.

WISCONSIN TERCENTENARY COMMEMORATIVE STAMP (3-CENT)—
ISSUE OF 1934

This stamp was issued to commemorate the three hundredth anniversary of the arrival of the French explorer, Jean Nicolet, on the shores of Green Bay, who, according to historical records, was the first white man to reach the territory now comprised in the State of Wisconsin.

The stamp is $^{84}/_{100}$ by $1^{44}/_{100}$ inches in dimension, arranged horizontally, and is inclosed within a narrow double-line border. It is printed in purple. Extending across the top of the stamp in a narrow panel with dark ground and white edges is the inscription "1634—Wisconsin Tercentenary—1934" in white Roman lettering. The central subject is reproduced from a painting depicting the arrival of the explorer. On a white ribbon panel at the base of the picture is the title "Nicolet's Landing on the Shores of Green Bay" in solid Gothic lettering. In a narrow panel, with white border that extends along the lower edge of the stamp, are the words "United States postage" in white Roman with small ornaments at either end. Resting on the base panel in each lower corner are dark rectangular panels with white edges inclosing the denomination designation "3¢" in white. Panels of the same width composed of fan-shaped ornaments extend to the top panel on each side.

The Wisconsin Tercentenary commemorative stamp was first offered for sale at the post office in Green Bay, Wis., on July 7, 1934.

NATIONAL PARKS POSTAGE STAMPS (1-CENT TO 10-CENT, INCLUSIVE)—ISSUE OF 1934

This special issue of ten postage stamps in denominations of 1 cent to 10 cents, inclusive, is the first series of stamps to be devoted entirely to scenic views from the national parks. The stamps were issued complimentary to the observance of 1934 as "National Parks Year."

The stamps of this series are of larger size, $^{84}/_{100}$ by $1^{44}/_{100}$ inches in dimension, in order to better accommodate the subject matter incorporated thereon. The stamps are issued in sheets of 50. The stamps of the different denominations are described as follows:

The 1-cent stamp is arranged vertically and is printed in green ink. This denomination shows a scene in Yosemite National Park with the famous El Capitan at the right. In a solid panel across the bottom of the stamp is the inscription "U. S. postage" in white Roman lettering. Resting on this base is a dark panel with curved top and ends, within which in a curved line along the upper edge is the title "Yosemite" in white Gothic. Below the title is the denomination designation "1¢" in white Roman flanked on either side by white-line ornaments. The stamp is inclosed in a narrow double-line border.

The 2-cent stamp is arranged horizontally and is printed in red ink. The central subject of this stamp is a view of the Grand Canyon, depicting the temples of Deva, Brahma, and Zoroaster, and Bright Angel Canyon. On either side of the stamp are upright panels containing the words "U. S. postage" at the left and "Grand Canyon" at the right in white Gothic letters arranged vertically within an ornamental framework. Within circular panels with white borders and solid background in each lower corner is the denomination designation "2¢" in white. The stamp is inclosed in a narrow double-line border.

The 3-cent stamp of this series is arranged horizontally and is inclosed in a narrow double-line border. A shadowed vertical panel at the right occupies approximately one-fifth of the area of the stamp. Within this panel at the top are the words "United States postage" in shaded Gothic lettering, arranged in three horizontal lines. Below this inscription and separated therefrom by a solid line ornament are the words "Three cents" in shaded Gothic, printed in two lines. Resting on an acanthus ornament at the bottom of this panel is a white disk containing a narrow double-line border within the outer circle. In the center of this disk is the solid Gothic numeral "3." The remaining space of the stamp at the left is a view of Mount Rainier with a reproduction of Mirror Lake in the foreground, in which the peak and surrounding trees are reflected. In a narrow panel at the base is the name "Mt. Rainier" in white Roman on a solid background. The stamp is printed in purple ink.

The 4-cent denomination is arranged horizontally and is printed in brown. The stamp is inclosed in a double-line border which is widened at the top and bottom of the stamp to form a narrow panel containing small arrowlike ornaments in white on a dark ground. The central subject is a view of the "Cliff Palace", one of the more important ruins of the prehistoric cliff dwellers in Mesa Verde National Park, Colo. At the base of the picture in a narrow panel with white edges and dark background is the title "Mesa Verde" in white Roman. In each lower corner is a rectangular panel, arranged vertically, with dark edges and white ground inclosing the large, dark numeral "4." Panels of the same width, with dark ground, extend to the top of the stamp on either side in which, arranged vertically, in white Gothic lettering are the words "U. S. postage" at the left and "Four cents" at the right.

The 5-cent stamp, arranged vertically, is inclosed in a narrow double-line border and is printed in blue ink. In a solid panel with white edges across the bottom of the stamp are the words "U. S. postage" in white Roman. Resting on this base is a lighter panel with curved top and ends, within which in a curved line near the top is the name "Yellowstone" in white Gothic. Below this title is the denomination designation "5¢", also in white Gothic, on either side of which appears a white-line ornament. The remaining space on the stamp is a reproduction of Old Faithful Geyser, one of the foremost scenic wonders of Yellowstone Park, with its column of hot water high in the air.

The 6-cent stamp, arranged horizontally, is inclosed in a narrow ruled panel border. A view of Crater Lake in Crater Lake National Park, showing portions of the surrounding rim and Wizard Island, occupies the major part of the space within the border. In a horizontal line in the upper central part of the stamp are the words "U. S. postage" in solid modified Gothic. In rectangular panels with light background and double-line borders in each lower corner is the denomination designation "6¢" in solid Gothic. In a narrow horizontal panel with light ground at the base of the stamp is the title "Crater Lake" in small dark Gothic letters. The stamp is printed in blue ink to conform to the color of the water in Crater Lake.

The 7-cent stamp is arranged horizontally, and has for the central design a view of Great Head, a rocky promontory on the shore of Acadia

National Park, Maine. At the bottom of the picture is the title "Acadia" in white Gothic letters. At each end of the stamp, in narrow upright panels with dark background bordered by paneling of lighter shade on either side, and with ornamental devices at the top and bottom, is the wording "U. S. postage" at the left and "Seven cents" at the right in white Gothic, arranged vertically. Within a circular panel with white ground, bordered by several dark lines, in the upper right corner of the space reserved for the central subject, is the denomination designation "7¢" in dark color. The stamp is printed in black ink.

The 8-cent denomination is arranged vertically and is enclosed in a narrow double-line border. It is printed in gray-green ink. The central design of this stamp is a reproduction of the "Great White Throne", one of the outstanding examples of the peculiar rock formations in Zion National Park, Utah. Below the picture is the title "Zion" in dark Gothic. In a narrow panel with white edges and dark ground along the base of the stamp are the words "U. S. postage" in white Roman lettering. The denomination designation "8¢" in dark color is shown in the upper right corner of the stamp.

The 9-cent stamp, arranged horizontally, is inclosed in a narrow double-line border and is printed in pink color. The central design depicts a scene from the Glacier National Park, showing lofty Mount Rockwell in the distance and Two Medicine Lake with bordering forest trees in the foreground. Arranged vertically at either end are ruled panels in which are inclosed other panels of lighter shade, with indented ends containing, at the left, the wording "U. S. postage", and "Glacier" at the right, all in solid Roman lettering. In the lower right corner is a small square with light background and double-line border inclosing the denomination designation "9¢" in dark color.

The 10-cent stamp is arranged vertically, and has for the central subject a view of Mount Le Conte, one of the outstanding points of interest in Smoky Mountain National Park. In a narrow panel across the top of the stamp, with dark ground, are the words "Great Smoky Mountains" in white Roman. In a similar panel at the base of the stamp are the words "United States postage" in white Roman. Resting on the base is a curved ribbon panel, in the central fold of which, on a light ground, is the word "Cents" in dark Roman. Immediately above, in a rectangular panel with dark ground, is the large numeral "10" in white Roman. The stamp is printed in slate-gray color.

The above stamps were first placed on sale as follows:

Denomination	Date	Post office
1-cent	July 16, 1934	Yosemite National Park, Calif.
2-cent	July 24, 1934	Grand Canyon, Ariz.
3-cent	Aug. 3, 1934	Longmire, Wash.
4-cent	Sept. 25, 1934	Mesa Verde National Park, Colo.
5-cent	July 30, 1934	Yellowstone Park, Wyo.
6-cent	Sept. 5, 1934	Crater Lake, Oreg.
7-cent	Oct. 2, 1934	Bar Harbor, Maine.
8-cent	Sept. 18, 1934	Zion National Park, Utah.
9-cent	Aug. 27, 1934	Glacier Park, Mont.
10-cent	Oct. 8, 1934	Gatlinburg, Tenn.

These stamps were also placed on sale the same dates at Washington, D. C.

SOUVENIR SHEET OF 3-CENT NATIONAL PARKS STAMPS—ISSUE OF 1934

The special sheet containing six stamps of the 3-cent Mount Rainier design of the National Parks series was authorized on behalf of the annual convention of the American Philatelic Society, held at Atlantic City, N. J., August 28 to September 1, 1934.

The sheet is printed in purple ink without perforations, but with the usual gumming. Sheets of this design were printed on the stamp press operated at the convention exhibition by the Bureau of Engraving and Printing. In the narrow margin on the four sides of the sheet in small Gothic lettering is the following wording: "Printed by the Treasury Department, Bureau of Engraving and Printing, under authority of James A. Farley, Postmaster

General, in compliment to the American Philatelic Society for its convention and exhibition, Atlantic City, N. J., August 1934."

This special sheet of stamps was first placed on sale August 28, 1934, at the branch Philatelic Agency, Atlantic City, which was operated in connection with the convention. This souvenir sheet was not issued to postmasters but it was made available for sale to collectors at the Philatelic Agency of the department, beginning September 4, 1934.

SOUVENIR SHEET OF 1-CENT NATIONAL PARKS STAMPS—ISSUE OF 1934

The department authorized the printing of a special sheet containing six of the 1-cent Yosemite National Parks stamps as a souvenir of the Trans-Mississippi Philatelic Exposition and Convention held in Omaha, Nebr., October 8 to 14, 1934.

The stamps are arranged on the sheet in 2 rows of 3 each. Each sheet is approximately 3⅝ inches wide by 3¾ inches high, and is gummed but not perforated. It is printed in green ink and with the following inscription on the four margins: "Printed by the Treasury Department, Bureau of Engraving and Printing, under authority of James A. Farley, Postmaster General, in compliment to the Trans-Mississippi Philatelic Exposition and Convention, Omaha, Nebraska, October 1934."

The special sheet of 1-cent Yosemite stamps was first placed on sale on October 10, 1934, at the temporary postal station of the Omaha post office operated in connection with the convention under the designation, "Trans-Mississippi Philatelic Convention Station."

For the benefit of other collectors, the souvenir sheet of 1-cent Yosemite stamps was placed on sale at the Philatelic Agency, Post Office Department, beginning October 15, 1934. This special issue of stamps was not placed on sale in post offices other than Omaha.

SPECIAL-DELIVERY AIR-MAIL POSTAGE STAMP (16-CENT)—ISSUE OF 1934

In this distinctive issue of postage stamps, provision was made for the payment of the postage and the special-delivery fee in one stamp. It represents the first combination stamp of this character ever issued by the department.

The new stamp is 8⁴⁄₁₀₀ by 1⁴⁴⁄₁₀₀ inches in dimension and is arranged horizontally. The stamp is inclosed in a narrow double-line border and is printed in blue ink. The central subject is a reproduction of the great seal of the United States of America. Across the top of the stamp are the words "Special Delivery" in white Roman lettering. On the sides of the stamp, arranged vertically, in white Gothic, are the words "U. S. postage" at the left, and "Air Mail" at the right. Along the bottom of the stamp, below the central design, is the word "Cents" in white Roman, on either side of which is the denomination designation "16."

The 16-cent special-delivery air-mail stamp was first offered for sale at the American Air Mail Society Convention Station, Chicago, Ill., on August 30, 1934.

SPECIAL ISSUE OF POSTAGE STAMPS IN UNCUT SHEETS AND BLOCKS—ISSUE OF 1935

A special issue of commemorative postage stamps in uncut sheets and blocks, in the denominations and varieties listed below, was authorized for the benefit of collectors and others interested:

3¢ Proclamation of Peace

Uncut sheets of 400 stamps (ungummed and *perforated*).
Blocks of 4 stamps (ungummed and *perforated*).

1¢ and 3¢ Century of Progress Souvenir Issue

Uncut sheets of 225 stamps (ungummed and unperforated).

3¢ Little America

Uncut sheets of 200 stamps (ungummed and *perforated*).
Blocks of 4 stamps (ungummed and *perforated*).

3¢ Little America Souvenir Issue

Uncut sheets of 150 stamps (ungummed and unperforated).

3¢ Mothers' (*Flat plate*)

Uncut sheets of 200 stamps (ungummed and unperforated).
Blocks of 4 stamps (ungummed and unperforated).

3¢ Wisconsin

Uncut sheets of 200 stamps (ungummed and unperforated).
Blocks of 4 stamps (ungummed and unperforated).

NATIONAL PARKS ISSUE

1¢, 2¢, 3¢, 4¢, 5¢, 6¢, 7¢, 8¢, 9¢, 10¢

Uncut sheets of 200 stamps (ungummed and unperforated).
Blocks of 4 stamps (ungummed and unperforated).

1¢ and 3¢ National Parks Souvenir Issue

Uncut sheets of 120 stamps (ungummed and unperforated).

16¢ Special-Delivery Air Mail

Uncut sheets of 200 stamps (ungummed and unperforated).
Blocks of 4 stamps (ungummed and unperforated).

These stamps were identical in design with those originally issued in sheet form and sold through post offices. The uncut sheets were sold intact as taken from the press, showing plate numbers, guide lines, etc. The special blocks of four stamps were trimmed to uniform size, which eliminated plate numbers.

These special uncut sheets and blocks of stamps were first made available at the Philatelic Agency, Post Office Department, Washington, D. C., on March 15, 1935, and were continued on sale until June 15, 1935. For the accommodation of collectors desiring first-day covers, the blocks of four of these stamps were also placed on sale at the post office at Washington, D. C., on March 15, 1935. They were not issued to other post offices.

CONNECTICUT TERCENTENARY COMMEMORATIVE STAMP—ISSUE OF 1935

This special postage stamp was issued in the 3-cent denomination to commemorate the three hundredth anniversary of the settlement of Connecticut. The stamp is $84/100$ by $144/100$ inches in dimension, arranged horizontally, and is inclosed within a single-line border. It is printed in rich lilac. The central design is a reproduction of the old historic Charter Oak. Across each end of the stamp are upright panels with light ground and dark edges containing the words "Connecticut" at the left and "Tercentenary" at the right, arranged vertically in architectural Roman lettering. In horizontal extensions of these panels at the top of the stamp are the dates "1635" at the left, and "1935" at the right, in dark figures. The lower edge of the top panel curves upward and forms a broad arch over the central design.

Within irregular-shaped panels in each lower corner, with light ground and dark edges, is the denomination designation "3¢" in dark color. In a narrow panel with dark ground, along the lower edge of the stamp are the words "United States postage" in white Gothic. Resting on the base panel and to the right of the center of the stamp is a narrow light ribbon panel containing the words "The Charter Oak" in dark Gothic lettering.

The Connecticut Tercentenary commemorative stamp was first offered for sale at the post office in Hartford, Conn., on April 26, 1935.

CALIFORNIA PACIFIC INTERNATIONAL EXPOSITION COMMEMORATIVE STAMP—ISSUE OF 1935

This special postage stamp in the 3-cent denomination was issued to commemorate the California Pacific International Exposition, which opened at San Diego, Calif., May 29, 1935.

The stamp is $84/100$ by $144/100$ inches in dimension, arranged horizontally, and is inclosed within a double-line border. The central subject of the stamp is a view of the exposition grounds, with Point Loma and San Diego Bay in the distance. In dark Gothic lettering, arranged in two horizontal lines at the top of the stamp, is the inscription "California Pacific International Exposition" above, and "1535—San Diego—1935" below. Within circular panels with dark background, in each lower corner, is the denomination designation "3¢", in white. In a narrow panel with dark background, at the base of the stamp, with white edges and ornamental device at each end are the words "U. S. postage" in white Roman lettering. The stamp is printed in purple ink.

The new stamp was first offered for sale at the post office in San Diego, Calif., on May 29, 1935.

BOULDER DAM COMMEMORATIVE STAMP—ISSUE OF 1935

This special postage stamp in the 3-cent denomination was issued to commemorate the completion of Boulder Dam.

The stamp is of the special delivery size, $^{84}/_{100}$ by $1^{44}/_{100}$ inches, arranged vertically, and is inclosed within a double line border. It is printed in purple ink. The central subject of the stamp is a view of Boulder Dam reproduced from an airplane picture taken at a low altitude, showing the river gorge both above and below the construction work. Across the bottom of the stamp is a white panel with the denomination designation "3¢" printed at each end. Along the base of this panel are the words "U. S. postage", in dark architectural Roman lettering. Above this inscription, within a narrow panel with white edges and dark background, is the wording "Boulder Dam—1935", in white Gothic lettering.

The new stamp was first offered for sale at the post office in Boulder City, Nev., on September 30, 1935.

MICHIGAN CENTENNIAL COMMEMORATIVE STAMP—ISSUE OF 1935

This special postage stamp in the 3-cent denomination was issued to commemorate the centennial anniversary of the Statehood of Michigan.

The stamp is of the special-delivery size, $^{84}/_{100}$ by $1^{44}/_{100}$ inches, arranged horizontally. It is surrounded by a double-line border and is printed in light purple. In a narrow panel with white edges and dark ground along the top edge of the stamp is the wording "1835 Michigan Centenary 1935", in white Roman. The central subject of the stamp is a large reproduction of the State seal, draped at the sides and base by the National Emblem at the left and the Michigan State banner at the right. The staffs of the flags extend to each upper corner. In square panels with dark ground in each lower corner is the denomination designation "3¢" in white. The wording "U. S. postage" in white Roman lettering is inclosed in a narrow horizontal panel with dark ground at the center of the lower edge of the stamp. In the space between the lower half of the central subject and the sides of the stamp is a forest and lake scene at the left, and at the right is a view representative of commerce and industry.

The new stamp was first offered for sale at the post office in Lansing, Mich., on November 1, 1935.

TRANS-PACIFIC AIR-MAIL STAMP—ISSUE OF 1935

This special stamp in the denomination of 25 cents was issued primarily for use on mail matter dispatched by the trans-Pacific air-mail service to Hawaii, Guam, and Philippine Islands. The new stamp is also valid for use on regular air mail.

The stamp is of the same size as the special-delivery stamp, $84\!/\!100$ by $144\!/\!100$ inches in dimension, arranged horizontally. It is surrounded by a double-line border and is printed in blue ink. In a narrow panel with white edges and dark ground across the top of the stamp is the wording, "Trans-Pacific Air Mail", in white Roman, with the date "November 1935" directly underneath in dark Gothic. In a horizontal panel with white edges and dark ground at the center of the lower margin of the stamp is the inscription reading "U. S. postage", in white Roman. In circular panels with white edges and dark ground in each lower corner of the stamp is the denomination designation "25¢" in white. Included in the central design is a representation of the sun rising from the shores of America, with a seaplane in flight over the ocean. At the right is pictured a modern ocean liner and at the left a Chinese junk, both partly obscured by the panels containing the denomination numeral. In the distance is a three-masted sailing vessel and a steamship representative of the middle nineteenth century period. The shield of the United States is shown at the upper left and that of the Philippine Islands at the upper right.

The new air-mail stamp was first placed on sale November 22, 1935, at the post offices in San Francisco, Calif., and Washington, D. C.

Collectors desiring covers between the designated points on the first trans-Pacific flight to and from Manila were permitted to send any desired number of envelopes bearing their home address under separate cover endorsed: "By First Contract Trans-Pacific Flight", to the postmasters at the respective offices, with remittance payable to the postmaster to cover the cost of the stamps required to be affixed thereto on a basis of the following rates:

	Number of stamps required	Cost per ½ ounce
		Cents
San Francisco to Hawaii	1	25
San Francisco to Guam	2	50
San Francisco to Manila	3	75
Hawaii to Guam	1	25
Hawaii to Manila	2	50
Guam to Manila	1	25

Each self-addressed envelope sent to these postmasters for dispatch by the first contract flight was required to bear an endorsement showing the scope of the service desired; for example, "San Francisco to Hawaii", "San Francisco to Philippine Islands", "Guam to San Francisco", etc. Upon arrival at the indicated destination such covers were continued in the mails to the addressee.

The Postmasters, San Francisco, Calif., and Washington, D. C., were authorized to comply with requests from collectors for first-day covers of the new air-mail stamp on November 22, to be sent by regular air mail direct to the addressee.

NEW ISSUE SPECIAL-DELIVERY AIR-MAIL STAMP—ISSUE OF 1936

This new issue of 16-cent special-delivery air-mail stamps was provided in bicolor to replace the stamp previously in use printed in blue ink.

The new stamp is $^{84}/_{100}$ by $1^{44}/_{100}$ inches in dimension, arranged horizontally, and is identical in design with the 16-cent special-delivery air-mail stamp issued on August 30, 1934, except for the reduction in size of the central subject and the printing of the stamp in two colors, the border in red and the central design, which is a reproduction of the Great Seal of the United States, in blue. This change in style was made in order that the stamp would be more distinctive and easily recognized, thereby contributing to the prompt and proper handling of such mail matter.

The bicolor 16-cent special-delivery air-mail stamp was first placed on sale at Washington, D. C., on February 10, 1936.

TEXAS CENTENNIAL COMMEMORATIVE STAMP—ISSUE OF 1936

This special postage stamp in the 3-cent denomination was issued to commemorate the centennial anniversary of Texas independence.

The stamp is of the same size as the special-delivery stamp, $^{84}/_{100}$ by $1^{44}/_{100}$ inches in dimension, arranged horizontally. It is inclosed in a double-line border, and is printed in purple. Within upright oval panels on either side of the stamp are portraits of Sam Houston at the left and Stephen F. Austin at the right, with their names in dark Gothic letters in narrow curved panels on white ground at the base of the ovals. In the upper central part of the stamp, partially superimposed over a large white star, is the inscription, "United States postage, Texas Centennial, 1836–1936", in dark Gothic, arranged in three horizontal lines. The lower part of the central design is a reproduction of the historic Alamo, with the title "The Alamo" in dark Gothic, in a narrow horizontal panel with white ground at the center of the lower edge of the stamp. The denomination designation "3¢" in dark lettering is shown in square panels with white ground in each lower corner of the stamp.

The new stamp was first offered for sale at the post office in Gonzales, Tex., on March 2, 1936.

RHODE ISLAND TERCENTENARY COMMEMORATIVE STAMP—ISSUE OF 1936

This special postage stamp in the 3-cent denomination was issued to commemorate the tercentenary anniversary of the founding of Rhode Island.

The stamp is the same size as the special-delivery stamp, $84\frac{1}{100}$ by $1^{44}\frac{1}{100}$ inches in dimension, arranged vertically. It is inclosed in a double-line border and is printed in purple. The words "U. S. postage" appear in dark Gothic lettering in a horizontal line at the top of the stamp, underneath which are the dates "1636" at the left and "1936" at the right in dark Gothic, between ornamental lines.

The central design is a likeness of Roger Williams modeled from a photograph of the statue in Roger Williams Park at Providence, R. I. The title "Roger Williams" appears on the base of the statue in dark Gothic. Between the base of the statue and the right side of the stamp is a circular panel with white ground inclosing the denomination designation "3¢" in dark lettering. In a corresponding position at the left is a reproduction of the central design of the State seal of Rhode Island. In a horizontal panel with white edges and dark ground at the base of the stamp, arranged in two lines, are the words "Rhode Island" above and "Tercentenary" below in white Roman lettering. The stamp was printed by the rotary process without straight edges and was issued in sheets containing 50 stamps.

The new stamp was first offered for sale at the post office in Providence, R. I., on May 4, 1936.

SOUVENIR SHEET OF 3-CENT POSTAGE STAMPS—ISSUE OF 1936

This special sheet containing four 3-cent stamps, embracing the Connecticut Tercentenary, California Pacific Exposition, and Michigan and Texas Centennial commemorative issues, was provided as a souvenir of the Third International Philatelic Exhibition of 1936, held in the Grand Central Palace, New York City, May 9 to 17, 1936.

The special stamp sheet is approximately 3⅝ inches wide and 2½ inches high, with the following inscriptions on the margins: "Printed by the Treasury Department, Bureau of Engraving and Printing", at the left; "Under Authority of James A. Farley, Postmaster General", at the top; "In Compliment to the Third International Philatelic Exhibition of 1936", at the right; and "New York, N. Y., May 9–17, 1936", at the lower edge. The sheet is printed in purple and was gummed but not perforated.

The souvenir sheet of four different issues of commemorative stamps was first placed on sale at the branch Philatelic Agency, Grand Central Palace, New York, N. Y., on May 9, 1936.

ARKANSAS CENTENNIAL COMMEMORATIVE STAMP—ISSUE OF 1936

This special postage stamp was issued in commemoration of the centennial anniversary of Arkansas statehood.

The stamp is the same size as the special-delivery stamp, $^{84}/_{100}$ by $1^{44}/_{100}$ inches in dimension, arranged horizontally. It is inclosed in a double-line border and is printed in purple. The central design of the stamp is a view of the old Statehouse, showing the portico of the central building and portion of the right wing, inclosed in a circular panel. On a white ribbon panel along the lower edge of the circle is the title "Old State House" in solid Gothic. At the left, partly below the central design, is a representation of the first settlement in Arkansas, above which appears the name "Arkansas Post" in solid Gothic, arranged in two lines. In a corresponding position at the right is pictured the present State capitol with the name above in dark Gothic in two lines. In each lower corner within circular panels, with double-line borders and solid ground, is the denomination numeral "3" in white architectural Roman. At the center of the lower edge of the stamp in a narrow horizontal panel with white edges and ornamental ends is the inscription "U. S. postage", and directly underneath "Three cents" in white Roman lettering. Arranged in solid Gothic lettering in the upper corners is the wording "Arkansas" at the left with the date "1836" below, and "Centennial" at the right with the date "1936" underneath. The stamp was printed by the rotary process without straight edges and was issued in sheets containing 50 stamps.

The new stamp was first offered for sale at the post office in Little Rock, Ark., on June 15, 1936.

OREGON TERRITORY COMMEMORATIVE POSTAGE STAMP—ISSUE OF 1936

This special postage stamp was authorized to commemorate the centennial anniversary of Oregon Territory.

The new stamp is the same size as the special-delivery stamp, $^{84}/_{100}$ by $1^{44}/_{100}$ inches in dimension, arranged horizontally. It is inclosed in a double-line border and is printed in purple. Within a horizontal panel with dark ground along the upper edge of the stamp is the wording "1836 Oregon Territory 1936" in white Roman lettering. The central design is a map of the old Oregon Territory comprising the present States of Idaho, Oregon, and Washington, together with parts of Montana and Wyoming. Marked on the map are the five places, one in each State, selected, for historical reasons, to have the first-day sale. There is also shown an outline of the old Oregon Trail.

In the vertical space between the ends of the rectangular panel containing the central design and the outer edge of the stamp there is, at the left, a western scene depicting a mounted Indian on a rocky promontory with wigwams on either side, behind which are shown trees and mountains. In a similar position at the right is portrayed a covered wagon train of the early pioneer days emerging from a pass in the mountains. The figures of the two front horses partly extend over the edge of the map panel.

In each lower corner is a circular panel with white edges and dark ground inclosing the large numeral "3" in white modernized Roman. In a narrow panel with dark ground along the lower edge of the stamp is the inscription "U. S. postage" and "Three cents" in white Roman, arranged in two lines. The lower line is extended by three white stars at either end. Short white lines with curved inner ends extend from lower corners of the map to the circles containing the denomination numeral. The stamp was printed by the rotary process without straight edges and was issued in sheets containing 50 stamps.

The stamp was first offered for sale at the following post offices on July 14, 1936: Lewiston, Idaho; Missoula, Mont.; Astoria, Oreg.; Walla Walla, Wash.; and Daniel, Wyo.

SUSAN B. ANTHONY COMMEMORATIVE POSTAGE STAMP—ISSUE OF 1936

This special postage stamp was issued in honor of Susan B. Anthony in connection with the sixteenth anniversary of the ratification of the nineteenth amendment granting suffrage to women.

The new stamp is of the ordinary size, $75/100$ by $87/100$ inch in dimension, arranged vertically. It is inclosed in a double-line border and is printed in purple. In a horizontal panel with dark ground across the top of the stamp is the wording, "U. S. postage" in white Roman. The central design is a portrait of Susan B. Anthony looking to the left. The portrait is inclosed in an oval frame with white edges and dark ground. On a curved ribbon with white ground at the base of the portrait is the name "Susan B. Anthony", in dark Gothic. In a narrow panel with dark ground along the lower edge of the stamp is the inscription reading "Suffrage for Women", in white Gothic. Immediately above, on either side, within circular panels with white edges and dark ground is the denomination designation "3¢" in white. The stamp was printed by the rotary process and was issued in sheets of 100 stamps.

The new stamp was first offered for sale at the Washington, D. C., post office on August 26, 1936.

ARMY AND NAVY COMMEMORATIVE STAMPS—ISSUE OF 1936-37

This special series of commemorative postage stamps will consist of five stamps for the Army in denominations of 1, 2, 3, 4, and 5 cents, and a like number in the same denominations for the Navy. Portraits of many noted military and naval leaders will appear on the stamps.

The 1-cent stamps of this special series were placed on sale in Washington, D. C., on December 15, 1936.

Both of the 1-cent stamps are of the special-delivery size, $84/100$ by $144/100$ inches in dimension, arranged horizontally in sheets of 50, printed by the rotary process. The stamps are inclosed in double-line borders and are printed in green.

On the 1-cent stamp of the Army series, inclosed in oval panels with light background that touch the top and side borders, are portraits of George Washington at the left and Nathanael Greene at the right. Beneath the ovals on white ribbons are the names "Washington" and "Greene" in dark Gothic. In the background between the ovals is a reproduction of Mount Vernon with the name below in dark Gothic. Within square panels in each lower corner with dark ground is the numeral "1" in white Roman. At the center of a narrow panel with dark ground along the base of the stamp are the words "One cent" in white Roman with laurel leaves on each side. Along the top and sides of the stamp, partly obscured by the oval frames, are narrow panels with white edges and dark ground, in the center of which, at 'the top, is the inscription "United States postage" in white Roman arranged in two lines. Below are sprays of laurel leaves that rise from behind the ovals. A five-pointed star in white is shown in both upper corners within small squares formed by the intersection of the inside lines of the top and side panels. The lower ends of the side panels inclose laurel branches.

The 1-cent stamp of the Navy series has for the central design, arranged in large ovals that touch the border at the top and sides, portraits of John Paul Jones at the left and John Barry at the right. In the background are depicted naval vessels of that period. On curved panels with white ground at the base of the ovals are the names "Jones" and "Barry", respectively, in dark Gothic. Below the portraits are the inscriptions *Bon Homme Richard* at the left, and *Lexington* at the right, in dark Gothic, representing famous naval vessels that were under their command. In a horizontal line between the ovals at the top of the stamp is the wording "United States postage" in dark Gothic. Within square panels with white edges and dark ground in each lower corner of the stamp is shown the numeral "1" in white Roman. At the center of a narrow panel with dark ground at the base of the stamp are the words "One cent" in white Roman with two five-pointed stars in white on each side.

SUMMARY

United States adhesive postage stamps were first issued under act of March 3, 1847, and placed on sale at New York, N. Y., July 1, 1847.

Books of stamps were first issued April 16, 1900.

Coils of stamps were first issued February 18, 1908.

Postal cards were first issued May 1, 1873, under act of June 8, 1872.

Stamped envelopes were first issued in June 1853, under act of August 30, 1852.

Printed stamped envelopes were first issued in the spring of 1865.

Newspaper wrappers were first issued in October 1861, under act of February 27, 1861.

Postage stamps have been issued in honor of the following Presidents and other persons prominent in American history:

PRESIDENTS

1. George Washington.
2. Thomas Jefferson.
3. James Madison.
4. James Monroe.
5. Andrew Jackson.
6. Zachary Taylor.
7. Abraham Lincoln.
8. Ulysses S. Grant.
9. Rutherford B. Hayes.
10. James A. Garfield.
11. Grover Cleveland.
12. Benjamin Harrison.
13. William McKinley.
14. Theodore Roosevelt.
15. Warren G. Harding.
16. Woodrow Wilson.
17. William H. Taft.

OTHER PROMINENT PERSONS

1. Benjamin Franklin.
2. Henry Clay.
3. Daniel Webster.
4. Winfield Scott.
5. Alexander Hamilton.
6. Oliver H. Perry.
7. Edwin M. Stanton.
8. William T. Sherman.
9. Columbus.
10. Queen Isabella.
11. John Marshall.
12. Father Marquette.
13. John C. Fremont.
14. Martha Washington.
15. David D. Farragut.
16. Robert R. Livingston.
17. Captain John Smith.
18. Pocahontas.
19. William H. Seward.
20. Balboa.
21. Nathan Hale.
22. John Ericsson.
23. Molly Pitcher.
24. George Rogers Clark.
25. General John Sullivan.
26. General Anthony Wayne.
27. Baron Steuben.
28. General Pulaski.
29. Count de Rochambeau.
30. Count de Grasse.
31. William Penn.
32. General Oglethorpe.
33. General Kosciusko.
34. Jean Nicolet.
35. Sam Houston.
36. Stephen F. Austin.
37. Roger Williams.
38. Susan B. Anthony.
39. John Barry.
40. John Paul Jones.
41. Nathanael Greene.

In addition to 11 separate series of ordinary postage stamps, special issues have been provided as follows:

Denomination	Quantity	Denomination	Quantity
COLUMBIAN EXPOSITION, ISSUE OF 1893		VICTORY, FOR ENDING OF WORLD WAR, ISSUE OF 1919	
1-cent	449, 195, 550	3-cent	99, 585, 200
2-cent	1, 464, 588, 750	PILGRIM TERCENTENARY, ISSUE OF 1920	
3-cent	11, 501, 250		
4-cent	19, 181, 550	1-cent	137, 978, 207
5-cent	35, 248, 250	2-cent	196, 037, 327
6-cent	4, 707, 550	5-cent	11, 321, 607
8-cent	10, 656, 550		
10-cent	16, 516, 950	HARDING MEMORIAL, ISSUE OF 1923	
15-cent	1, 576, 950		
30-cent	617, 250	Flat	1, 459, 487, 085
50-cent	243, 750	2-cent { Rotary	99, 950, 300
$1	55, 050	Imperf	770, 000
$2	45, 550	HUGUENOT-WALLOON TERCENTENARY, ISSUE OF 1924	
$3	27, 650		
$4	26, 350	1-cent	51, 378, 023
$5	27, 350	2-cent	77, 753, 423
TRANS-MISSISSIPPI (OMAHA) EXPOSITION, ISSUE OF 1898		5-cent	5, 659, 023
		ONE HUNDRED AND FIFTIETH ANNIVERSARY, BATTLE OF LEXINGTON AND CONCORD, ISSUE OF 1925	
1-cent	70, 993, 400		
2-cent	159, 720, 800		
4-cent	4, 924, 500	1-cent	15, 615, 000
5-cent	7, 694, 180	2-cent	26, 596, 600
8-cent	2, 927, 200	5-cent	5, 348, 800
10-cent	4, 629, 760	NORSE-AMERICAN CENTENNIAL ANNIVERSARY, ISSUE OF 1925	
50-cent	530, 400		
$1	56, 900	2-cent	9, 104, 983
$2	56, 200	5-cent	1, 900, 983
PAN-AMERICAN EXPOSITION, ISSUE OF 1901		SESQUICENTENNIAL OF AMERICAN INDEPENDENCE, ISSUE OF 1926	
1-cent	91, 401, 500		
2-cent	209, 759, 700	2-cent	307, 731, 900
4-cent	5, 737, 100	ERICSSON MEMORIAL, ISSUE OF 1926	
5-cent	7, 201, 300		
8-cent	4, 921, 700	5-cent	20, 280, 500
10-cent	5, 043, 700	BATTLE OF WHITE PLAINS, ISSUE OF 1926	
LOUISIANA PURCHASE EXPOSITION, ISSUE OF 1904			
		2-cent	40, 639, 485
1-cent	79, 779, 200	2-cent (panes of 25) 107,398	2, 684, 950
2-cent	192, 732, 400	LINDBERGH AIR MAIL, ISSUE OF 1927	
3-cent	4, 542, 600		
5-cent	6, 926, 700	10-cent	20, 379, 179
10-cent	4, 011, 200	10-cent (in books of 6)	873, 360
TERCENTENARY OF FOUNDING OF JAMESTOWN, ISSUE OF 1907		BURGOYNE CAMPAIGN, ISSUE OF 1927	
1-cent	77, 728, 794	2-cent	25, 628, 450
2-cent	149, 497, 994	VERMONT SESQUICENTENNIAL, ISSUE OF 1927	
5-cent	7, 980, 594		
ONE HUNDREDTH ANNIVERSARY, BIRTH OF ABRAHAM LINCOLN, ISSUE OF 1909		2-cent	39, 974, 900
		VALLEY FORGE SESQUICENTENNIAL, ISSUE OF 1928	
Perf	148, 387, 191	2-cent	101, 330, 328
2-cent { Imperf	1, 273, 900	HAWAII SESQUICENTENNIAL, ISSUE OF 1928	
Blue paper	637, 000		
ALASKA-YUKON-PACIFIC EXPOSITION, ISSUE OF 1909		2-cent	5, 519, 897
		5-cent	1, 459, 897
2-cent { Perf	152, 887, 311	BATTLE OF MONMOUTH SESQUICENTENNIAL, ISSUE OF 1928	
Imperf	525, 400		
HUDSON-FULTON ANNIVERSARY, ISSUE OF 1909		2-cent	9, 779, 896
		INTERNATIONAL CIVIL AERONAUTICS CONFERENCE, ISSUE OF 1928	
2-cent { Perf	72, 634, 631		
Imperf	216, 480	2-cent	51, 342, 273
PANAMA-PACIFIC, ISSUE OF 1913		5-cent	10, 319, 700
1-cent	334, 796, 926		
2-cent	503, 713, 086		
5-cent	29, 088, 726		
10-cent	16, 968, 365		

Denomination	Quantity	Denomination	Quantity
GEORGE ROGERS CLARK EXPEDITION, ISSUE OF 1929		OLYMPIC WINTER GAMES, ISSUE OF 1932	
2-cent	16, 684, 674	2-cent	51, 102, 800
FIFTIETH ANNIVERSARY OF FIRST ELECTRIC LIGHT, ISSUE OF 1929		ARBOR DAY ANNIVERSARY, ISSUE OF 1932	
2-cent { Flat	31, 679, 200	2-cent	100, 869, 300
Rotary	210, 119, 474		
Coils	133, 530, 000	XTH OLYMPIC GAMES, ISSUE OF 1932	
SULLIVAN EXPEDITION, ISSUE OF 1929		3-cent	168, 885, 300
2-cent	51, 451, 880	5-cent	52, 376, 100
BATTLE OF FALLEN TIMBERS ANNIVERSARY, ISSUE OF 1929		ONE HUNDRED AND FIFTIETH ANNIVERSARY, BIRTH OF DANIEL WEBSTER, ISSUE OF 1932	
2-cent	29, 338, 274	3-cent	49, 538, 500
OHIO RIVER CANALIZATION, ISSUE OF 1929		TWO HUNDRED AND FIFTIETH ANNIVERSARY, ARRIVAL OF WILLIAM PENN IN AMERICA, ISSUE OF 1932	
2-cent	32, 680, 900		
MASSACHUSETTS BAY TERCENTENARY, ISSUE OF 1930		3-cent	49, 949, 000
2-cent	74, 000, 774	GENERAL OGLETHORPE COMMEMORATIVE STAMP, ISSUE OF 1933	
FOUNDING OF PROVINCE OF CAROLINA AND CITY OF CHARLESTON, ISSUE OF 1930		3-cent	61, 719, 200
2-cent	25, 215, 574	PROCLAMATION OF PEACE, ISSUE OF 1933	
GRAF ZEPPELIN AIR MAIL STAMP, ISSUE OF 1930		3-cent { Regular	73, 382, 400
65-cent	93, 536	Uncut sheets or 400___ 7, 585	3, 034, 000
$1.30	72, 428	Uncut blocks of 4___ 60, 139	240, 556
$2.60	61, 296	CENTURY OF PROGRESS, ISSUE OF 1933	
BATTLE OF BRADDOCK ANNIVERSARY, ISSUE OF 1930			
2-cent	25, 609, 470	1-cent { Regular	348, 266, 800
TWO HUNDREDTH ANNIVERSARY, BIRTH OF GENERAL VON STEUBEN, ISSUE OF 1930		Souvenir panes of 25_ 456, 704	11, 417, 600
		Uncut souvenir panes_ 10, 968	2, 467, 800
		3-cent { Regular	480, 239, 300
2-cent	66, 487, 000	Souvenir panes of 25_ 441, 172	11, 029, 300
ONE HUNDRED AND FIFTIETH ANNIVERSARY, DEATH OF GENERAL PULASKI, ISSUE OF 1931		Uncut souvenir panes_ 9, 546	2, 147, 850
2-cent	96, 559, 400	N. R. A. EMERGENCY POSTAGE STAMP, ISSUE OF 1933	
FIFTIETH ANNIVERSARY, AMERICAN RED CROSS, ISSUE OF 1931		3-cent	1, 978, 707, 300
2-cent	99, 074, 600	GENERAL KOSCIUSKO COMMEMORATIVE POSTAGE STAMP, ISSUE OF 1933	
YORKTOWN SESQUICENTENNIAL, ISSUE OF 1931			
2-cent	25, 006, 400	5-cent	45, 137, 700
GEORGE WASHINGTON BICENTENNIAL ANNIVERSARY, ISSUE OF 1932		GRAF ZEPPELIN AIR MAIL STAMP, ISSUE OF 1933	
½-cent	87, 969, 700	50-cent	324, 070
1-cent	1, 265, 555, 100	LITTLE AMERICA, ISSUE OF 1933	
1½-cent	304, 926, 800	3-cent { Regular	5, 735, 944
2-cent	4, 222, 198, 300	Souvenir panes of 6_ 811, 404	4, 868, 424
3-cent	456, 198, 500	Uncut sheets of 200__ 8, 942	1, 788, 400
4-cent	151, 201, 300	Uncut blocks of 4___ 63, 090	252, 360
5-cent	170, 565, 100	Uncut souvenir panes_ 10, 688	1, 603, 200
6-cent	111, 739, 400	MARYLAND TERCENTENARY COMMEMORATIVE POSTAGE STAMP, ISSUE OF 1934	
7-cent	83, 257, 400		
8-cent	96, 506, 100		
9-cent	75, 709, 200	3-cent	46, 258, 300
10-cent	147, 216, 000		

Denomination	Quantity	Denomination	Quantity
COMMEMORATIVE STAMP IN HONOR OF MOTHERS, ISSUE OF 1934		**CONNECTICUT TERCENTENARY, ISSUE OF 1935**	
3-cent Regular {Flat	15,432,200	3-cent	70,726,800
Regular {Rotary	193,239,100	**SAN DIEGO EXPOSITION, ISSUE OF 1935**	
Uncut sheets of 200__ 10,391	2,078,200	3-cent	[1] 100,000,000
Uncut blocks of 4____ 77,772	311,088		
WISCONSIN TERCENTENARY ISSUE OF 1934		**BOULDER DAM, ISSUE OF 1935**	
3-cent {Regular	64,525,400	3-cent	73,610,650
Uncut sheets of 200__ 9,958	1,991,600	**MICHIGAN CENTENARY, ISSUE OF 1935**	
Uncut blocks of 4____ 75,837	303,348	3-cent	[1] 75,823,900
NATIONAL PARKS, ISSUE OF 1934		**TEXAS CENTENNIAL, ISSUE OF 1936**	
1-cent {Regular	84,896,350	3-cent	[1] 125,000,000
Souvenir panes of 6__ 793,551	4,761,306	**RHODE ISLAND TERCENTENARY, ISSUE OF 1936**	
Uncut sheets of 200__ 14,415	2,883,000	3-cent	67,127,650
Uncut blocks of 4____ 83,659	334,636	**SOUVENIR SHEET, THIRD INTERNATIONAL PHILATELIC EXHIBITION, ISSUE OF 1936**	
Uncut sou. panes____ 13,998	1,679,760	3-cent panes of 4_____ 2,809,039	11,236,156
2-cent {Regular	74,400,200	**ARKANSAS CENTENNIAL, ISSUE OF 1936**	
Uncut sheets of 200__ 12,119	2,423,800	3-cent	[1] 75,000,000
Uncut blocks of 4____ 80,710	322,840	**OREGON TERRITORY, ISSUE OF 1936**	
3-cent {Regular	95,089,000	3-cent	[1] 75,000,000
Souvenir panes of 6__ 511,391	3,068,346	**SUSAN B. ANTHONY, ISSUE OF 1936**	
Uncut sheets of 200__ 9,397	1,879,400	3-cent	[1] 200,000,000
Uncut blocks of 4____ 72,172	288,688	**ARMY AND NAVY SERIES, ISSUE OF 1936-37**	
Uncut sou. panes____ 10,796	1,295,520	1-cent (Army)	[1] 100,000,000
4-cent {Regular	19,178,650	1-cent (Navy)	[1] 100,000,000
Uncut sheets of 200__ 7,716	1,543,200		
Uncut blocks of 4____ 69,871	279,484		
5-cent {Regular	30,980,100		
Uncut sheets of 200__ 7,270	1,454,000		
Uncut blocks of 4____ 67,644	270,576		
6-cent {Regular	16,923,350		
Uncut sheets of 200__ 6,943	1,388,600		
Uncut blocks of 4____ 64,774	259,096		
7-cent {Regular	15,988,250		
Uncut sheets of 200__ 7,125	1,425,000		
Uncut blocks of 4____ 64,487	257,948		
8-cent {Regular	15,288,700		
Uncut sheets of 200__ 6,930	1,386,000		
Uncut blocks of 4____ 63,161	252,644		
9-cent {Regular	17,472,600		
Uncut sheets of 200__ 6,868	1,373,600		
Uncut blocks of 4____ 62,906	251,624		
10-cent {Regular	18,874,300		
Uncut sheets of 200__ 6,958	1,391,600		
Uncut blocks of 4__ 63,325	253,300		

[1] Ordered.

117210°—37——8

Denomination	Quantity	Denomination	Quantity
MISCELLANEOUS ISSUES		STATE SURCHARGED STAMPS, ISSUE, OF 1929	
AIR MAIL STAMPS, REGULAR SERIES		Kansas	
Issue of 1918:		1-cent	13, 390, 000
6-cent	3, 395, 854	1½-cent	8, 240, 000
16-cent	3, 793, 887	2-cent	87, 410, 000
24-cent	2, 134, 888	3-cent	2, 540, 000
Issue of 1923:		4-cent	2, 290, 000
8-cent	6, 414, 576	5-cent	2, 700, 000
16-cent	5, 309, 275	6-cent	1, 450, 000
24-cent	5, 285, 775	7-cent	1, 320, 000
Issue of 1928:		8-cent	1, 530, 000
5-cent (bicolor)	106, 887, 675	9-cent	1, 130, 000
Issue of 1930:		10-cent	2, 860, 000
5-cent ⎰Flat	97, 641, 200	Nebraska	
Issue of 1932: ⎱Rotary	57, 340, 050	1-cent	8, 220, 000
8-cent	76, 648, 803	1½-cent	8, 990, 000
Issue of 1934:		2-cent	73, 220, 000
⎧Special-delivery air-mail (regular)	9, 215, 750	3-cent	2, 110, 000
		4-cent	1, 600, 000
16-cent⎨Uncut sheets of 200 ____ 5, 734	1, 146, 800	5-cent	1, 860, 000
		6-cent	980, 000
⎪Uncut blocks of		7-cent	850, 000
⎩4 ____ 55, 940	223, 760	8-cent	1, 480, 000
		9-cent	530, 000
		10-cent	1, 890, 000

PLATES USED IN PRINTING COMMEMORATIVE AND AIR-MAIL POSTAGE STAMPS

COLUMBIAN EXPOSITION, ISSUE OF 1893

1-cent: J–46 to 50, K–51 to 55, P–65 to 69, MM–149 to 153, OO–159 to 163, VV–194 to 198. (Total, 30 plates.)

2-cent: 100 subjects, F–26 to 30, G–31 to 35, H–36 to 40, I–41 to 45, O–60 to 64, Q–70 to 74, U–83 to 87, X–94 to 98, GG–119 and 123; 200 subjects, A–1 to 5, C–11 to 15, E–21 to 25, T–78 to 82, V–88 to 92, EE–109 to 113, FF–114 to 118, HH–124 to 128, JJ–134 to 138, KK–139 to 143, LL–144 to 148, NN–154 to 158, PP–164 to 168, QQ–169 to 173, RR–174 to 178, SS–179 to 183, TT–184 to 188, UU–189 to 193. (Total, 132 plates.)

3-cent: L–56, L–57, R–75, R–76. (Total, 4 plates.)

4-cent: D–16 to 20. (Total, 5 plates.)

5-cent: B–6 to 10. (Total, 5 plates.)

6-cent: Z–104. (Total, 1 plate.)

8-cent: II–129 to 133. (Total, 5 plates.)

10-cent: Y–99 to 103. (Total, 5 plates.)

15-cent: M–58. (Total, 1 plate.)

30-cent: N–59. (Total, 1 plate.)

50-cent: S–77. (Total, 1 plate.)

$1: W–93. (Total, 1 plate.)

$2: AA–105. (Total, 1 plate.)

$3: BB–106. (Total, 1 plate.)

$4: CC–107. (Total, 1 plate.)

$5: DD–108. (Total, 1 plate.)

TRANS-MISSISSIPPI, ISSUE OF 1898

1-cent: *590*, 91, 92; *598*, *600*, 01; *605; 607; 612; 635; 709*, 10, 11, 12. (Total, 14 plates.)

2-cent: *597; 608; 610*, 11; *615*, 16; *619; 621*, 22, 23, 24, 25, 26, 27, 28, 29, 30, 31, 32, 33; *638*, 39, 40, 41, 42; *644*, 45, 46, 47, 48, 49, 50, 51, 52, 53, 54, 55, 56, 57, 58, 59, 60, 61, 62, 63, 64, 65, 66, 67, 68, 69, 70, 71, 72, 73, 74, 75, 76, 77, 78, 79, 80, 81; *683*, 84, 85, 86, 87, 88, 89, 90, 91, 92, 93, 94, 95, 96, 97, 98, 99; *700*, 01, 02, 03, 04, 05, 06, 07, 08; *713*, 14, 15, 16, 17, 18, 19, 20, 21, 22; *724*, 25, 26, 27, 28, 29; *732*, 33, 34, 35; *737*, 38, 39, 40, 41, 42, 43, 44; *749*, 50, 51, 52.   (Total, 121 plates.)
4-cent: *599, 634, 636*.   (Total, 3 plates.)
5-cent: *602, 614, 618*.   (Total, 3 plates.)
8-cent: *609, 643*.   (Total, 2 plates.)
10-cent: *604, 617, 620*.   (Total, 3 plates.)
50-cent: *603*.   (Total, 1 plate.)
$1: *606*.   (Total, 1 plate.)
$2: *613*.   (Total, 1 plate.)

PAN-AMERICAN, ISSUE OF 1901

1-cent: *1112; 1116; 1123; 1139; 1172; 1175; 1179; 1181*, border; *1113; 1117; 1125; 1136; 1156; 1168; 1170; 1177; 1180; 1194; 1196; 1225*, 26, 27, 28; *1233*, 34, 35; *1248*, center.   (Total, 9 plates, border; 20 plates, center.)
2-cent: *1078; 1092; 1098; 1114; 1119; 1122; 1126; 1129; 1165; 1167; 1169; 1176*, border; *1079; 1093; 1115; 1118; 1124; 1127*, 28; *1134*, 35; *1137*, 38; *1166; 1171; 1173*, 74; *1178; 1182; 1187; 1192*, 93; *1195; 1197*, 98; *1208; 1221*, 22, 23, 24; *1229*, 30, 31, 32; *1238*, 39, 40, 41, center.   (Total, 12 plates, border; 36 plates, center.)
4-cent: *1145*, border; *1142*, center.   (Total, 1 plate, border; 1 plate, center.)
5-cent: *1140*, border; *1141*, center.   (Total, 1 plate, border; 1 plate, center.)
8-cent: *1150*, border; *1143*, center.   (Total, 1 plate, border; 1 plate, center.)
10-cent: *1151*, border; *1144*, center.   (Total, 1 plate, border; 1 plate, center.)

LOUISIANA PURCHASE, ISSUE OF 1904

1-cent: *2113*, 14, 15, 16, 17, 18, 19, 20; *2129*, 30, 31, 32; *2137*, 38, 39, 40; *2149*, 50, 51, 52; *2161*, 62, 63, 64.   (Total, 24 plates.)
2-cent: *2069*, 70, 71, 72; *2081*, 82, 83, 84; *2093*, 94, 95, 96; *2125*, 26, 27, 28; *2145*, 46, 47, 48; *2153*, 54, 55, 56, 57, 58, 59, 60; *2165*, 66, 67, 68; *2177*, 78, 79, 80; *2182*, 83, 84, 85.   (Total, 40 plates.)
3-cent: *2101*, 02, 03, 04.   (Total, 4 plates.)
5-cent: *2097*, 98, 99; *2100*.   (Total, 4 plates.)
10-cent: *2105*, 06, 07, 08.   (Total, 4 plates.)

JAMESTOWN, ISSUE OF 1907

1-cent: *3538; 3540*, 41, 42, 43, 44, 45, 46; *3799*.   (Total, 9 plates.)
2-cent: *3504*, 05; *3512*, 13; *3517; 3520; 3522; 3524; 3577*, 78, 79, 80; *3592*, 93, 94, 95; *3601*, 02, 03, 04; *3610; 3613; 3618*, 19; *3655*, 56, 57, 58; *3671*, 72; *3677*, 78. (Total, 32 plates.)
5-cent: *3554; 3556; 3560*, 61.   (Total, 4 plates.)

LINCOLN MEMORIAL, ISSUE OF 1909

2-cent: *4976*, 77, 78, 79; *4981*, 82, 83, 84.   (Total, 8 plates.)

ALASKA-YUKON-PACIFIC, ISSUE OF 1909

2-cent: *5142*, 43, 44, 45; *5170*, 71, 72, 73; *5208*, 09, 10, 11; *5235*, 36, 37; *5241; 5249*, 50, 51; *5257*.   (Total, 20 plates.)

HUDSON-FULTON, ISSUE OF 1909

2-cent: *5388*, 89, 90, 91, 92, 93, 94, 95.   (Total, 8 plates.)

PANAMA-PACIFIC, ISSUE OF 1912–13

1-cent: *6127*, 28; *6131*, 32; *6144; 6146*, 47, 48; *6548*, 49, 50, 51; *6875; 6880; 6891; 6944.*   (Total, 16 plates.)

2-cent: *6306*, 07, 08, 09, 10, 11, 12, 13, 14, 15, 16, 17; *6320*, 21, 22, 23; *6432; 6442; 6447; 6647*, 48, 49, 50; *7034*, 35; *7038*, 39.   (Total, 27 plates.)

5-cent: *6129; 6133*, 34; *6138*.   (Total, 4 plates.)

10-cent: *6130; 6135; 6139; 6143*.   (Total, 4 plates.)

VICTORY, ISSUE OF 1919

3-cent: *9412*, 13, 14, 15, 16, 17, 18, 19; *9426*, 27, 28, 29, 30, 31, 32, 33.   (Total, 16 plates.)

PILGRIM TERCENTENARY, ISSUE OF 1920

1-cent: *12418*, 19, 20, 21; *12428*, 29; *12431; 12436*, 37, 38, 39; *12448*.   (Total, 12 plates.)

2-cent: *12422*, 23, 24, 25; *12432*, 33, 34, 35; *12440*, 41, 42, 43, 44, 45, 46, 47; *12452*, 53, 54, 55.   (Total, 20 plates.)

5-cent: *12426*, 27.   (Total, 2 plates.)

HARDING MEMORIAL, ISSUE OF 1923 (FLAT)

2-cent: *14852*, 53, 54, 55, 56, 57, 58, 59, 60, 61, 62, 63; *14868*, 69, 70, 71, 72, 73, 74, 75, 76, 77, 78, 79; *14884*, 85, 86, 87, 88, 89, 90, 91, 92, 93, 94, 95, 96, 97, 98, 99; *14902*, 03, 04, 05, 06, 07, 08, 09; *14940*, 41, 42, 43; *14946*, 47, 48, 49; *14954*, 55, 56; *14972; 14987*, 88, 89, 90, 91, 92, 93, 94; *14997*, 98, 99; *15000; 15005*, 06, 07, 08, 09, 10, 11, 12; *15017*, 18, 19, 20; *15025*, 26, 27, 28, 29, 30, 31, 32; *15035*, 36, 37, 38, 39, 40, 41, 42; *15053*, 54, 55, 56, 57, 58, 59, 60, 61, 62, 63, 64, 65, 66, 67, 68; *15077*, 78, 79, 80, 81, 82, 83, 84; *15089*, 90, 91, 92; *15097*, 98, 99; *15100; 15109*, 10, 11, 12, 13, 14, 15, 16, 17, 18, 19, 20, 21, 22; *15129*, 30, 31, 32; *15137*, 38, 39; *15155*, 56, 57, 58; *15163*, 64, 65; *15167; 15177; 15178; 15191*, 92; *15195*. (Total, 166 plates.)

The following flat plates were *not used: 14957; 15123*, 24; *15140; 15166; 15168*, 69, 70; *15175; 15189*, 90; *15196*, 97, 98; *15202; 15208*, 09, 10.   (Total unused, 18 plates.)

Rotary: *14866*, 67; *14900*, 01; *14938*, 39; *14995*, 96.   (Total, 8 plates.)

The following rotary plates were *not used: 15001*, 02; *15013*, 14.   (Total unused, 4 plates.)

HUGUENOT-WALLOON, ISSUE OF 1924

1-cent: *15756*, 57, 58, 59; *15778*, 79, 80, 81, 82, 83, 84, 85.   (Total, 12 plates.)

2-cent: *15744*, 45, 46, 47; *15760*, 61, 62, 63; *15766*, 67, 68, 69; *15786*, 87, 88, 89. (Total, 16 plates.)

5-cent: *15752*, 53, 54, 55.   (Total, 4 plates.)

LEXINGTON-CONCORD, ISSUE OF 1925

1-cent: *16797*, 98, 99; *16800*.   (Total, 4 plates.)

2-cent: *16801; 16803*, 04; *16813*, 14, 15, 16; *17004*.   (Total, 8 plates.)

5-cent: *16805*, 06, 07, 08.   (Total, 4 plates.)

NOT USED

1-cent: *16817*, 18, 19, 20; *16922*, 23.   (Total, 6 plates.)
2-cent: *17005*, 06.   (Total, 2 plates.)
5-cent: *16918*, 19.   (Total, 2 plates.)

NORSE-AMERICAN, ISSUE OF 1925

2-cent: *16924; 16694; 16958*, 59, border.   (Total, 4 plates.)   *16687*, 88, 89; 16960;
17353; 17355, 56; 17379, center.   (Total, 8 plates.)
5-cent: *16925*, 26; *10961; 16963*, border.   (Total, 4 plates.)   *16927*, 28, 29; *16957*,
center.   (Total, 4 plates.)

PHILADELPHIA SESQUI-CENTENNIAL, ISSUE OF 1926

2-cent: *18540*, 41, 42, 43, 44, 45, 46, 47; *18552*, 53, 54, 55, 56, 57, 58, 59, 60, 61,
62, 63, 64, 65, 66, 67, 68, 69, 70, 71, 72, 73, 74, 75, 76, 77, 78, 79, 80, 81, 82, 83;
18634, 35, 36, 37, 38, 39, 40, 41; *18646*, 47, 48, 49, 50, 51, 52, 53; *18664*, 65,
66, 67.   (Total, 60 plates.)

JOHN ERICSSON, ISSUE OF 1926

5-cent: *18595; 18597*, 98, 99; *18600*, 01; *18606*, 07, 08, 09; *18612*, 13.   (Total,
12 plates.)

BATTLE OF WHITE PLAINS, ISSUE OF 1926

2-cent: *18765*, 66, 67, 68, 69, 70, 71, 72, 73, 74.   (Total, 10 plates.)   (Plate no.
18772 was used at the International Exposition in New York City, but none
of the stamps printed from it were placed on sale.)

VERMONT, ISSUE OF 1927

2-cent: *19035*, 36, 37, 38, 39, 40, 41, 42.   (Total, 8 plates.)

BURGOYNE, ISSUE OF 1927

2-cent: *19061*, 62, 63, 64, 65, 66, 67, 68, 69; *19106*.   (Total, 10 plates.)

VALLEY FORGE, ISSUE OF 1928

2-cent: *19493*, 94, 95, 96, 97; *19500*, 01, 02.   (Total, 8 plates.)   *Not used: 19503;*
19525, 26, 27, 28.

HAWAIIAN, ISSUE OF 1928

2-cent: *18983*, 84; *19054*, 55.   (Total, 4 plates.)
5-cent: *18907*, 08.   (Total, 2 plates.)

BATTLE OF MONMOUTH, ISSUE OF 1928

2-cent: *19070*, 71.   (Total, 2 plates.)

INTERNATIONAL CIVIL AERONAUTICS CONFERENCE, ISSUE OF 1928

2-cent: *19654*, 55, 56, 57; *19662*, 63, 64, 65; *19678*, 79, 80, 81; *19708*, 09, 10, 11.
(Total, 16 plates.)
5-cent: *19658*, 59, 60, 61.   (Total, 4 plates.)

GEORGE ROGERS CLARK, ISSUE OF 1929

2-cent: *19720*, 21, 22, 23, 24, 25, 26, 27; *19740*, 41, 42, 43, border. (Total, 12 plates.) *19728*, 29, 30, 31, 32, 33, 34, 35, 36, 37, 38, 39, center. (Total, 12 plates.)

THOMAS ALVA EDISON, ISSUE OF 1929

2-cent: *19775*, 76, 77, 78, flat. (Total, 4 plates.) *19779*, 80; *19796*, 97; *19806*, 07, 08, 09, rotary. (Total, 8 plates.) *19781*, 82; *19794*, 95; *19802*, 03, 04, 05, 170—subject (coils).

SULLIVAN EXPEDITION, ISSUE OF 1929

2-cent: *19783*, 84, 85, 86. (Total, 4 plates.) Not used: *19787; 19798*, 99; *19800*, 01.

BATTLE OF FALLEN TIMBERS, ISSUE OF 1929

2-cent: *19824*, 25, 26, 27, 28, 29, 30, 31. (Total, 8 plates.)

OHIO RIVER CANALIZATION, ISSUE OF 1929

2-cent: *19838*, 39, 40, 41; *20005*. (Total, 5 plates.)

MASSACHUSETTS BAY COLONY, ISSUE OF 1930

2-cent: *20053*, 54, 55, 56, 57, 58, 59, 60. (Total, 8 plates.)

CHARLESTON, S. C., ISSUE OF 1930

2-cent: *20061*, 62, 63, 64. (Total, 4 plates.) Not used: *20065*, 66, 67, 68.

BATTLE OF BRADDOCK'S FIELD, ISSUE OF 1930

2-cent: *20168*, 69, 70, 71. (Total, 4 plates.)

GENERAL BARON VON STEUBEN, ISSUE OF 1930

2-cent: *20267*, 68, 69, 70; *20281*, 82, 83, 84. (Total, 8 plates.)

GENERAL PULASKI, ISSUE OF 1931

2-cent: *20416*, 17, 18, 19, 20, 21, 22, 23, 24, 25, 26, 27. (Total, 12 plates.)

RED CROSS, ISSUE OF 1931

2-cent: *20434*, 35, 36, 37, 38, 39, 40, 41; *20450*, 51, 52, 53, 54, 55, 56, 57; *20466*, 67, 68, 69; *20514*, 15, 16; *20525*. *Black.* (Total, 24 plates.)
20445, 46, 47, 48, 49; *20489*, 90, 91, 92, 93, 94, 95, 96, 97, 98, 99; *20500*, 01, 02, 03. *Red.* (Total, 20 plates.)
Not used, black: *20513; 20526*, 27, 28. (Total, 4 plates.) Red: *20442*, 43, 44; *20517*, 18, 19, 20, 21, 22, 23, 24. (Total, 11 plates.)

YORKTOWN, ISSUE OF 1931

2-cent: *20461*, 62, 63, 64, 65; *20478*, 79, 80, 81, 82, 83, 84, 85, 86, 87, 88; *20668*, 69, 71; *20646*, 47, 48, 49, border. (Total, 24 plates.)
20470; *20472*, 73, 74, 75, 76, 77; *20504*, 05, 06, 07, 08, 09, 10, 11, 12; *20597*, 98, 99; *20600*, 01, 02; *20650*, 51, 52, 53; *20656*, 57, 58, 59; *20660*; *20662*, 63; *20665*, 66, 67, center. (Total, 36 plates.)
Not used, border: *20458*, 59, 60; *20485*, 86, 87, 88, 89; *20490*, 91, 92. (Total, 11 plates.) Center: *20471; 20603*, 04. (Total, 3 plates.)

George Washington Bicentennial, Issue of 1932

½-cent: *20559*, 60; *20605; 20629; 20698*, 99. (Total, 6 plates.) *Not used: 20700*, 01; *20769*, 70.

1-cent: *20561*, 62; *20573*, 74; *20654*, 55; *20690*, 91, 92, 93; *20714*, 15; *20739*, 40, 41, 42; *20747; 20766; 20775*, 76; *20831*, 32; *20835*, 36; *20839*, 40; *20843*, 44. (Total, 28 plates.) *Not used: 20748; 20765*. (Total, 2 plates.)

1½-cent: *20632*, 33, 34, 35; *20678*, 79, 80, 81. (Total, 8 plates.) *Not used: 20833*, 34; *20837*, 38.

2-cent: *20555*, 56; *20577*, 78; *20583*, 84; *20630*, 31; *20644*, 45; *20685; 20696*, 97; *20706*, 07; *20716*, 17; *20726*, 27; *20733*, 34; *20749*, 50, 51, 52, 53, 54, 55, 56; *20759*, 60, 61, 62, 63, 64; *20767*, 68; *20771*, 72, 73, 74; *20781*, 82, 83, 84; *20789*, 90, 91, 92, 93, 94, 95, 96; *20801*, 02, 03, 04, 05, 06; *20684*. (Total, 60 plates.) *Not used: 20811*, 12, 13, 14; *20827*, 28, 29, 30. (Total, 8 plates.)

3-cent: *20557*, 58; *20694*, 95; *20847*, 48; *21014*, 15; *21042*, 43, 44, 45. (Total, 12 plates.) *Not used: 21054*, 55, 56, 57, 58, 59. (Total, 6 plates.)

4-cent: *20567*, 68; *20593*, 94. (Total, 4 plates.)

5-cent: *20636*, 37, 38, 39. (Total, 4 plates.) *Not used: 20682*, 83. (Total, 2 plates.)

6-cent: *20569*, 70. (Total, 2 plates.) *Not used: 20718*, 19. (Total, 2 plates.)

7-cent: *20563*, 64; *20731*, 32. (Total, 4 plates.)

8-cent: *20565*, 66. (Total, 2 plates.) *Not used: 20735*, 36. (Total, 2 plates.)

9-cent: *20640*, 41. (Total, 2 plates.) *Not used: 20737*, 38. (Total, 2 plates.)

10-cent: *20642*, 43; *20686*, 87. (Total, 4 plates.) *Not used: 20757*, 58. (Total, 2 plates.)

Third Winter Olympic Games, Issue of 1932

2-cent: *20815*, 16, 17, 18, 19, 20, 21, 22, 23, 24, 25, 26. (Total, 12 plates.)

Arbor Day, Issue of 1932

2-cent: *20872*, 73, 74, 75, 76, 77. (Total, 6 plates.)

Tenth Olympiad, Issue of 1932

3-cent: *20864*, 65; *20906*, 07, 08, 09. (Total, 6 plates.)

5-cent: *20868*, 69, 70, 71. (Total, 4 plates.) *Not used: 20866*, 67. (Total, 2 plates.)

William Penn, Issue of 1932

3-cent: *21064*, 65, 66, 67, 68, 69, 70, 71, 72, 73, 74, 75. (Total, 12 plates.)

Daniel Webster, Issue of 1932

3-cent: *21034*, 35, 36, 37, 38, 39, 40, 41; *21046*, 47, 48, 49. (Total, 12 plates.)

General Oglethorpe, Issue of 1933

3-cent: *21096*, 97, 98, 99; *21100*, 01, 02, 03, 04, 05, 06, 07, 08, 09, 10, 11. (Total, 16 plates.)

Proclamation of Peace, Issue of 1933

3-cent: *21118*, 19, 20, 21; *21123*, 24. (Total, 6 plates.)

Century of Progress, Issue of 1933

1-cent: *21131*, 32, 33, 34, 35, 36; *21139*, 40, 41, 42. (Total, 10 plates.)

3-cent: *21125*, 26, 27, 28, 29, 30; *21137*, 38. (Total, 8 plates.)

SPECIAL IMPERFORATE SHEETS OF 25, UNGUMMED

1-cent: *21145*, used at Chicago; *21159*, used at Bureau of Engraving. *Not used: 21143.*

3-cent: *21146*, used at Chicago, *21160*, used at Bureau of Engraving. *Not used: 21144.*

. N. R. A. EMERGENCY, ISSUE OF 1933

3-cent: *21151*, 52, 53, 54, 55, 56, 57, 58; *21161*, 62, 63, 64, 65, 66. (Total, 14 plates.)

LITTLE AMERICA, ISSUE OF 1933

3-cent: *21167*, 68, 69, 70. (Total, 4 plates.)

SPECIAL SHEETS OF SIX, IMPERFORATE AND UNGUMMED

3-cent: *21184*, used at Bureau of Engraving; *21187*, used at New York Exhibition. (Total, 2 plates.)

GENERAL KOSCIUSKO, ISSUE OF 1933

5-cent: *21173*, 74, 75, 76. (Total, 4 plates.)

MARYLAND TERCENTENARY, ISSUE OF 1934

3-cent: *21188*, 89, 90, 91; *21196*, 97, 98, 99. (Total, 8 plates.)

MOTHERS OF AMERICA, ISSUE OF 1934

3-cent: *21202*, 03, 04, 05, *flat*. (Total, 4 plates.) *21210*, 11, 12, 13, 14, 15, 16, 17, 18, 19, *rotary*. (Total, 10 plates.)

WISCONSIN TERCENTENARY, ISSUE OF 1934

3-cent: *21238*, 39, 40, 41, 42, 43, 44, 45. (Total, 8 plates.)

NATIONAL PARKS, ISSUE OF 1934

1-cent: *21246*, 47, 48, 49, 50, 51, 52, 53. (Total, 8 plates.) Special imperforate sheets of six, gummed: *21341*. (Total, 1 plate.)

2-cent: *21254*, 55, 56, 57, 58, 59, 60, 61. (Total, 8 plates.)

3-cent: *21262*, 63, 64, 65; *21332*; *21274*, 75, 76, 77. (Total, 9 plates.) Special imperforate sheets of six, gummed: *21303*. (Total, 1 plate.)

4-cent: *21328*, 29, 30, 31. (Total, 4 plates.)

5-cent: *21278*, 79, 80, 81. (Total, 4 plates.)

6-cent: *21320*, 21, 22, 23. (Total, 4 plates.)

7-cent: *21333*, 34, 35, 36. (Total, 4 plates.)

8-cent: *21324*, 25, 26, 27. (Total, 4 plates.)

9-cent: *21316*, 17, 18, 19. (Total, 4 plates.)

10-cent: *21337*; *21339*, 40; *21342*. (Total, 4 plates.)

SPECIAL UNCUT SHEETS OF STAMPS, ISSUE OF 1935

Proclamation of Peace:
    3-cent: *21118*, 19. (Total, 2 plates.)

Century of Progress:
    1-cent: *21145*; *21159*. (Total, 2 plates.)
    3-cent: *21146*; *21160*. (Total, 2 plates.)

Little America:
    3-cent: *21167*, 68, 69, 70. (Total, 4 plates.)

Little America souvenir sheet:
    3-cent: *21184*. (Total, 1 plate.)
Mothers of America (flat):
    3-cent: *21202*, 03, 04, 05. (Total, 4 plates.)
Wisconsin:
    3-cent: *21238*, 39, 40, 41. (Total, 4 plates.)
National Parks:
    1-cent: *21246*, 47, 48, 49. (Total, 4 plates.)
    2-cent: *21254*, 55, 56, 57. (Total, 4 plates.)
    3-cent: *21262*, 63, 64, 65. (Total, 4 plates.)
    4-cent: *21328*, 29, 30, 31. (Total, 4 plates.)
    5-cent: *21278*, 79, 80, 81. (Total, 4 plates.)
    6-cent: *21320*, 21, 22, 23. (Total, 4 plates.)
    7-cent: *21333*, 34, 35, 36. (Total, 4 plates.)
    8-cent: *21324*, 25, 26, 27. (Total, 4 plates.)
    9-cent: *21316*, 17, 18, 19. (Total, 4 plates.)
    10-cent: *21337*; *21339*, 40; *21342*. (Total, 4 plates.)
National Parks souvenir sheets:
    1-cent: *21341*. (Total, 1 plate.)
    3-cent: *21303*. (Total, 1 plate.)
Air mail—special delivery:
    16-cent: *21312*, 13, 14, 15. (Total, 4 plates.)

CONNECTICUT TERCENTENARY, ISSUE OF 1935

3-cent: *21391*, 92, 93, 94, 95, 96. (Total, 6 plates.)

CALIFORNIA PACIFIC INTERNATIONAL EXPOSITION, ISSUE OF 1935

3-cent: *21405*, 06, 07, 08, 09; *21410*. (Total, 6 plates.)

BOULDER DAM, ISSUE OF 1935

3-cent: *21455*, 56, 57, 58, 59; *21460*, 61, 62, 63, 64, 65, 66. (Total, 12 plates.)

MICHIGAN CENTENNIAL, ISSUE OF 1935

3-cent: *21467*; *21469*; *21470*, 71. Not used: *21468*; *21472*. (Total, 4 plates.)

TEXAS CENTENNIAL, ISSUE OF 1936

3-cent: *21537*, 38, 39, 40. (Total, 4 plates.)

RHODE ISLAND TERCENTENARY, ISSUE OF 1936

3-cent: *21559*, 60, 61, 62. (Total, 4 plates.)

THIRD INTERNATIONAL PHILATELIC EXHIBITION, SOUVENIR SHEET, ISSUE OF 1936

3-cent: *21557*, *21558*. (Total, 2 plates.)

ARKANSAS CENTENNIAL, ISSUE OF 1936

3-cent: *21564*, 65, 66, 67. (Total, 4 plates.)

OREGON TERRITORY, ISSUE OF 1936

3-cent: *21576*, 77, 78, 79. (Total, 4 plates.)

Susan B. Anthony, Issue of 1936

3-cent: *21588*, 89; *21590*, 91.   (Total, 4 plates.)

Air Mail, Issue of 1918

6-cent: *9155*.   (Total, 1 plate.)
16-cent: *8900*.   (Total, 1 plate.)
24-cent: *8492*, border.   (Total, 1 plate.)   *8493*, center.   (Total, 1 plate.)

Air Mail, Issue of 1923

8-cent: *14824*, 25, 26, 27.   (Total, 4 plates.)
16-cent: *14828*, 29, 30, 31.   (Total, 4 plates.)
24-cent: *14840*, 41, 42, 43.   (Total, 4 plates.)

Air Mail, Issue of 1926–27

10-cent: *18246*, 47, 48, 49, 50; *18903*, 04, 05.   (Total, 8 plates.)
15-cent: *18745*, 46, 47, 48.   (Total, 4 plates.)
20-cent: *18890*, 91, 92, 93, 94; *18897*, 98, 99.   (Total, 8 plates.)

Air Mail, Lindbergh, Issue of 1927

10-cent: *18997*, 98, 99; *19000*, 01, 02, 03, 04, 05, 06, 07, 08.

Lindbergh Booklet

10-cent: *19414; 19425*, 26, 27.

Air Mail, Issue of 1928

5-cent: *19549*, 50, 51, 52; *19565*, 66, 67, 68, 69, 70, 71, 72; *19585*, 86, 87, 88, 89, 90, 91, 92; *19605*, 06, 07; *19612*, 13, 14, 15; *19620*, 21, 22, 23, 24, 25, 26, 27, 28, 29, 30, 31, 32, 33, 34, 35; *19670*, 71, 72, 73; *19696*, 97, 98, 99; *19700*, 01, 02, 03, border.   (Total, 55 plates, border.)   *19545*, 46, 47, 48; *19573*, 74, 75, 76, 77, 78, 79, 80; *19597*, 98, 99; *19600; 19608*, 09, 10, 11; *19616*, 17, 18, 19; *19636*, 37, 38, 39; *19666*, 67, 68, 69; *19674*, 75, 76, 77; *19688*, 89, 90, 91, 92, 93, 94, center.   (Total, 43 plates, center.)

Air Mail, Issue of 1930

5-cent: *19941*, 42, 43, 44, 45, 46, 47, 48; *20187*, 88, 89, 90; *20323*, *flat*.   (Total, 13 plates.)
5-cent: *20606*, 07, *rotary*.   (Total, 2 plates.)

Graf Zeppelin

65-cent: *20077*, 78, 79, 80.   (Total, 4 plates.)
$1.30: *20085*, 86, 87, 88.   (Total, 4 plates.)
$2.60: *20089*, 90, 91, 92; *20095*.   (Total, 5 plates.)

Air Mail, Issue of 1932

8-cent: *21028*, 29, 30, 31, 32, 33.   (Total, 6 plates.)

Air Mail, Issue of 1933

ZEPPELIN

50-cent: *21171*, 72; *21177*, 78.   (Total, 4 plates.)

AIR MAIL, ISSUE OF 1934

6-cent: *21234*, 35, 36, 37.   (Total, 4 plates.)

SPECIAL-DELIVERY AIR MAIL, ISSUE OF 1934

16-cent: *21312*, 13, 14, 15.   (Total, 4 plates.)

TRANS-PACIFIC AIR MAIL, ISSUE OF 1935

25-cent: *21473*, 74, 75, 76.   (Total, 4 plates.)

SPECIAL-DELIVERY AIR MAIL, ISSUE OF 1936

(BICOLOR)

16-cent: Frame (red): *21491*, 92, 93, 94.   (Total, 4 plates).   Center (blue): *21495*, 96, 97, 98, 99; *21500*, 01, 02.   (Total, 8 plates.)

○

www.ingramcontent.com/pod-product-compliance
Lightning Source LLC
Chambersburg PA
CBHW061958040426
42447CB00010B/1802